SYSTEMATIC THEOLOGY TODAY:
THE STATE OF THE ART IN NORTH AMERICA

Part I

Thor Hall

University Press of America™

Copyright © 1978 by

University Press of America, Inc.™

4710 Auth Place, S.E., Washington, D.C. 20023

Printed in the United States of America

ISBN: 0-8191-0645-3

Library of Congress Catalog Card Number: 78-70520

This volume represents the result of a study which was begun in the spring of 1974 under a project entitled "The Present State of the Discipline of Systematic Theology." This project was undertaken in response to several felt needs: the need for an up-to-date picture of the discipline, of those who are involved in it, and of what is being done within it; and the need for this picture to be based on information that is broadly representative, that comes from the grass roots of the discipline, not simply from observers or commentators, market analysts among publishers or trend setters among editors. Our aim was, first , to identify all active professional systematic theologians in the United States and Canada (Protestant and Catholic, though primarily scholars and teachers, located in colleges, universities, seminaries, or church institutes); secondly, to obtain from each person the relevant information concerning his or her background, training, careers, and current activities (teaching, research, and publications), as well as responses to a number of questions related to the evaluation of the current state of the arts in the discipline; and finally, to publish this material, partly in the form of a DIRECTORY OF SYSTEMATIC THEOLOGIANS IN NORTH AMERICA, and partly in the form of an analytical summary entitled THE STATE OF THE ARTS IN NORTH AMERICAN SYSTEMATIC THEOLOGY TODAY.

The DIRECTORY, containing all the factual information we have gathered and presenting it in the form of biographical summaries of each individual scholar in the field, was published under the auspices of The Council on the Study of Religion in the spring of 1977. The analytical summary, based partly on the material included in the DIRECTORY and partly on a vast number of responses we have received in answer to certain evaluative questions included in our questionnaire, is presented in part here. Together, these two publications provide the most inclusive, up-to-date picture of the present state of affairs in North-American systematic theology available anywhere today. Part II of this work is to appear next year.

The introduction, below, describes the project, the research procedures, and the process by which this volume has come into being. It parallels, at several points, the opening chapter in the DIRECTORY, but it completes the picture of our project and serves as the final report on the undertaking, both for the benefit of colleagues who are interested in the techniques involved and for the benefit of those who have supported the project, financially and otherwise, and who would want to know what has been done during the three years of its duration. The Introduction is quite detailed and specific. This is for a particular purpose. If the people interested in the discipline of systematic theology find the results of this study to be as valuable as we think they are, scholars concerned to analyze the present state of affairs in other disciplines of study, and especially in other areas of religious studies, might also find themselves inspired to undertake similar projects; they will then be able to learn some things about the undertaking in a vicarious manner, not having to recapitulate the trials and errors which we have had to face.

Now that this project is completed, I would like to acknowledge my indebtedness to a number of people, individuals as well as groups. The University of Tennessee at Chattanooga has provided me the opportunity to engage in this kind of work. The University Administration, and the Faculty Research Committee handling the applications for research grants funded by the University of Chattanooga Foundation, has supported the project since its inception. Additional funding has come from the Benwood Foundation of Chattanooga. Colleagues in the Department of Philosophy and Religion, and in other departments, have given unstinting support and valuable help all along. Major credit for the completion of the project is due to Mrs. June Breland, my research assistant and secretary, who with persistence and patience has handled all the details, collated all the information, and typed most of the original manuscript. The Department Secretary, Mrs. Judy Beebe, and several student assistants have made significant contributions also. Mrs. Valerie H. Johnson typed the book as it appears here. I thank them all, as I do my wife Gerd, without whose faithful presence and constant interest I would not be sustained for any accomplishments.

I must also recognize the help and cooperation which I have received from Dr. Norman E. Wagner and Dr. Harold Remus, Executive Directors of the Council on the Study of Religion, and from the Research and Publications Committee of the Council. The Council has for some time been interested in projects designed as inventories of academic disciplines; the decision of the Committee to sponsor the publication of the DIRECTORY was an encouragement along the way for which I am most grateful. I appreciate also the support and cooperation of the University Press of America in publishing this present volume and in producing it so quickly.

Finally, and most obviously, I am of course indebted to the many colleagues in the discipline who conscientiously responded to our inquiries, filled out our questionnaire, and liberally shared their thoughts and opinions with us. Many of them are quoted in the chapters to follow. All of them are part of the profile of our discipline which is outlined in this book.

I trust that they will recognize themselves and find their views responsibly presented. Perhaps more important yet, I hope that they will find their self-understanding as systematic theologians deepened, as I have, by being portrayed together with the whole family.

Chattanooga, summer of '78
T. H.

Contents

Introduction

Systematic Theologians: Getting to Know Them

Whenever anyone is called upon to comment on the theological situation today he is likely to have a difficult time deciding what to talk about. For one thing, if he is looking for dominant figures, individual scholars who are considered leading lights in the field, he will find them hard to identify and his choices even harder to defend. For another, if he is trying to discover prevailing trends or schools of thought that can be isolated and analyzed, bracketed and identified, he will find himself confronted with such a multitude of orientations that the subject most closely resembles the proverbial can of worms.

The judgment most commentators come up with, when they do decide to say something, is therefore likely to be of the following two varieties: either that theology is "in the doldrums," "between times," "without leadership," or "floundering," or that it is "in upheaval," "characterized by experimentation," "confusing," or "confused."

Both of these judgments are suppo.table. No one who knows anything about theology in the twentieth century can avoid noticing that the first two thirds of the century were marked by the presence of giants—and an impressive number of them at that. At the beginning of the century, there was a Harnack and a Schweitzer; soon there emerged a Barth, a Bultman, a Brunner; then came the Scandinavians, Aulen, Nygren, and the Americans, the Niebuhrs, Tillich. But by the end of the second third of the century, the great masters of the age were either gone or going, and no one seemed ready to assume the role. One could perhaps point to a number of pretenders—in Germany, a Rahner, a Küng, a Moltmann, a Pannenberg; in Scandinavia, a Wingren, a Prenter; in Britain, a Torrance, a Robinson; and in America, a Lonergan, a Cox, a Cobb, a Cone—but in comparison with the giants of the earlier generation they are revealed to be no more than that—pretenders. It seems unlikely that any one of them will rise to the kind of prominence, or preeminence, which marked their illustrious predecessors.

When one looks at contemporary theology, attempting to identify not individual leaders but current trends, one is faced with a literal profusion of perspectives, orientations, methodologies, and language games. A list of theologies presently propounded reveals both the high creativity and

3

imagination and the broad complexity and confusion which has taken hold of the theological community--if it can be called a community any more. There are theologies of biography, black liberation, change, culture, death of God, ecumenics, fantasy, freedom, history, holocaust, hope, humor, imagination, joy, liberation, love, mystery, myth, narrative, oppression, paradox, peace, personality, play, politics, process, psychotherapy, revolution, sensibility, story, symbol, tradition, transcendence, women's liberation, et cetera--each representing a different point of view, and each laying claim to priority on the agenda of the theologians of the day. And the possibilities for additions and variations seem unlimited; new theological trends are apparently as inexhaustible as the inventiveness of the human mind itself. There are always candidates waiting in the wings to audition some new act and sign themselves up with the managers and promoters in the market place.

The difficulty which besets those who would want to describe the theological situation today by reference to the leading lights or the latest trends is that the named few may not be altogether representative of the unnamed many, and that the latest trends may turn out to be no more than waves, not major currents. Theology, I would propose, is rather analogous to an iceberg. The shapes and configurations which appear above water reveal precious little about the rest of the massive entity which floats, below the surface, deep in the ocean; and the winds and waves which swirl about on top say nothing about the direction of the drift, determined as that is by the stronger currents below. Yet what is happening in theology is often described simply by reference to and from the perspective of the visible tip of the iceberg.

Personally, I have never been able to answer confidently the question which as a theologian I am time and again called upon to answer, "What is happening in theology these days?" For me to answer this question responsibly, I have felt, much more would be involved than going to professional conferences, keeping up with the journals, checking publishers' catalogues, and reading books and book reviews. There is so much more to the discipline--the many disciplines--of theology than that which surfaces on the breakers at the society beaches and the literary oceanfront. Trying to describe the theological situation on the basis of such impressions and observations would be quite as hazardous as if an oceanographer were to speculate about what is happening in the deep blue seas, having no more evidence than that which can be gathered along the beaches on his afternoon strolls. If one really wants to know what is going on in the ocean one must get out on it and down in it; and if one really is to describe what is happening in theology one must inquire very broadly among the practitioners of the art, the professionals in the field, the rank and file. Or so it seems to me.

4

It was under the impact of these and similar feelings that I decided, four years ago, to undertake a thorough study of my own particular discipline, systematic theology. The immediate concern was to identify the people who are actively and professionally involved in the discipline, primarily in North America (United States and Canada). Secondly, I wanted to know as much about them as possible, about their background and training, their careers and present positions, and about their current activities and future plans. Then, thirdly, I was anxious to learn their views and thoughts on a number of questions related to the discipline, how they interpret the present situation, how they conceive of the task ahead, how they define their own method, and what are the main emphases in their work. The project was entitled, "The Present State of the Discipline of Systematic Theology in North America." The ultimate objective was to publish two sources that would make the material gathered available to the theological community at large; one a DIRECTORY OF SYSTEMATIC THEOLOGIANS IN NORTH AMERICA, a factual record containing relevant information on each individual scholar who is an active participant in the discipline; the other, an analytical review of the discipline, including the self-interpretation of those presently involved in it, entitled THE STATE OF THE ARTS IN NORTH AMERICAN SYSTEMATIC THEOLOGY TODAY.

The rest of this introduction is the story of this project, and the rest of this book Part I of the analytical overview.

Getting Organized

To begin with the project did not appear to be as complex and time consuming as it turned out to be. In fact, in the early sketches of the plan we identified three phases in the undertaking, a) data gathering, b) categorization and analysis, and c) editing and manuscript preparation, and we estimated that a reasonable time frame for the whole project would be a little more than 12 months. As it turned out, each of the three phases proved to take that much time by itself; the whole project, four years.

We began the work in January 1974 with two major assets; one a $2,000 grant from the Faculty Research Committee of the University of Tennessee at Chattanooga; the other a part-time research assistant and secretary specifically assigned to this project. With the availability of additional student assistants we thought ourselves in good shape.

Our first task was to build a complete roster of all active professional systematic theologians in the United States and Canada. No such
roster existed; we needed one that included Protestants and Catholics,
teachers, scholars and writers, in colleges, universities, seminaries and
institutes, wherever employed and of whatever background. I had corres-
ponded earlier with the Executive Director of the Council on the Study of
Religion--the coordinating council of all professional societies in the field
of religious studies--to inquire if the membership lists of these societies in
any way identified the disciplines of study in which the members are involved. The answer was that they did not, but that the Council had recently
distributed a questionnaire throughout the constituencies of the member
societies, requesting each member to indicate by way of certain broad
categories the fields of study in which he or she is primarily interested.
The responses had not yet been processed. The council was waiting for a
decision from the National Endowment for the Humanities on a grant application which had been submitted on behalf of a so-called "inventory
project"--a comprehensive survey of scholarship, discipline by discipline,
across the whole field of religious studies. However, for a small fee a research assistant could sort out the forms of those members who had indicated
an interest in theology, philosophy of religion, and related fields, and
these could be sent us on loan for a time. We decided to accept this offer,
but to use the inventory information only in a supplementary manner and as
an auxiliary source. Frankly, the categories utilized in the CSR questionnaire appeared to us to be too broad for our purposes. We needed information that would lead us to the people who identify themselves as systematic
theologians more directly.

Our first step was to make inquiries with the primary institutions
where systematic theologians were most likely to be located, namely theological seminaries and graduate schools. From the Association of American
Theological Schools we obtained a current list of member institutions,
AATS DIRECTORY OF THEOLOGICAL SCHOOLS, and proceeded to write
each of them, first the accredited member schools, then the associate member schools, requesting copies of their latest catalogue. As these were received, we checked carefully the lists of active faculty members and began
to build a card file with names of people listed as having primary responsibilities in theology, most immediately systematic theology, but including
also persons whose responsibilities were described in correlative terms such
as dogmatics, philosophical theology, history of doctrine, and moral theology. We were not at the time concerned to define or delimit the discipline too narrowly; we would rather rely on the self-understanding of scholars to guide us in determining who were involved in systematic theology
and who were not.

We went next to the DIRECTORY OF RELIGIOUS STUDIES PROGRAMS AND DEPARTMENTS OF RELIGION IN NORTH AMERICA, compiled by Professor Robert Wright and published by CSR in 1973, singling out all departments and programs listed as offering "theology" or "systematic theology" as an area of specialization. Letters of inquiry were sent to the heads of such departments and programs, requesting that they provide us the names of all faculty members involved in these areas of study and teaching. We were well aware that this DIRECTORY listing was incomplete, and that systematic theologians might well be found in colleges and universities which offered no specific programs or concentrations in these fields, and we decided therefore to augment our roster by other means.

At this point the CSR "inventory" questionnaires were of considerable value to us. We collated the questionnaires with our own roster, adding the names of people who had indicated an interest in "theology," "systematic theology," or any correlative field of study, and who were not already included. In addition, shortly after we went public with our inquiries, we published a note on the project in the CSR BULLETIN, requesting that anyone who considered himself involved in the discipline of systematic theology, but who had not yet been contacted, write us for information and copies of our questionnaire.

As the result of all these inquiries a card file of some 1,230 names and addresses was eventually assembled. We proceeded to correspond with everyone included on our roster.

In developing the plans for our project we had in mind, of course, some general conceptions of the kinds of information we would need from each person. By the time our roster was completed this had all been crystallized into a specific research instrument, a questionnaire--together with personally addressed covering letter--which was distributed by first class mail. Since our interests were partly to obtain biographical and factual information related to the publication of a DIRECTORY, and partly to gather opinions and interpretations relative to the analysis of the present state of the discipline of systematic theology, we had developed a questionnaire which provided room for listing a series of personal and professional facts as well as for answering a series of questions related to the evaluation of the discipline. The specific categories for listing the factual information focused on such things as name, address, current position, year of birth, years of teaching, years in current affiliation, as well as certain questions concerning academic background, professional career, teaching responsibilities, research interests, publications, and active research projects. The evaluative questions ranged over a wide spectrum, from "How

would you describe the current state of the discipline of systematic theology" and "What in your view is the main task facing the systematic theologian in the foreseeable future," to "Which of the major theologians of
the past do you consider closest to your own position," "How would you
describe your own theological method," and "What are the most important emphases in your own work?"

One major issue which had to be settled in connection with the
formulation of the questionnaire had to do with the definition and delim-
itation of the discipline of systematic theology itself. We were aware of
a number of equivocations in the way theologians and theological institutions used the term; we were conscious, also, of the need to determine the
relationship between systematic theology, however defined, and the correlative subject areas of "theological methodology," "principles of theology,"
"dogmatics," "symbolics," "history of doctrine," "fundamental theology,"
"constructive theology," and "philosophical theology."

In studying the general use of the term "systematic theology" we
found evidence of two prevalent, even predominant trends. Some circles
were found to use the phrase in a narrow sense, referring to the systematic
and integrated explication of basic Christian doctrines; others were observed to use the term more broadly, referring to an inclusive and integrating
study of the entire system of Christian faith--a study which involved a
whole spectrum of subsidiary disciplines, from philosophical and biblical
studies, as well as dogmatic and historical studies, to moral theology and
practical, pastoral theology as well. Both of these usages have their
background in tradition and both of them involve problems. The broad
definition has obviously been difficult to maintain. It presupposes that the
systematic theologian is knowledgeable in every field of theological study--
philosophical, biblical, dogmatic, historical, and practical--and implies
that systematic theology is in some sense the queen of the theological
sciences, with the other disciplines serving more or less as the handmaids
of the systematicians--all of which is liable to be judged quite presump-
tuous by colleagues in the "subsidiary" disciplines and likely to be proven
less and less feasible as the specialization and the complexity of these
disciplines increases. But the narrower definition has had its difficulties
as well. If systematic theology is defined in an exclusive sense, in contra-
distinction to philosophical, biblical, historical, or practical theology,
the discipline is in some danger of losing the interdisciplinary quality
which is essential to the fulfillment of its function, namely the systematic
exposition of the total complex of Christian faith. Set apart in such splendid isolation, the systematic theologian is likely to find it even harder to
define what his particular function, sources and methods are.

8

In view of the equivocations and differences of opinions that existed both with regard to the use of the term and in connection with the conception of the discipline itself, we decided to use such formulations in our questionnaire as would not capriciously prejudge the issue or cause anyone who is interested in systematic theology, however defined, to feel excluded. Our cover letter stated the matter as follows:

> As you may expect, one major problem in a project such as this is the delimination of the discipline of "systematic theology" itself. Some use this term rather narrowly, others with wider reference. In the questionnaire (III,1,b) we have indicated that both a wider reference and a narrower concept are relevant to our study. We shall include, therefore, those who are interested in "principles of theology" (methodology), "dogmatics" (history of doctrine, symbolics), "systematic theology" narrowly defined (constructive, philosophical theology), as well as those engaged in "other," more specific subject areas (such as moral theology, contemporary theology, etc.).

In formulating the questionnaire itself we consequently included the entire spectrum and provided space for indicating which of these interests were included in the respondent's own work area. Those who understood themselves as systematic theologians in the stricter sense would thus be able to check the particular category described as "systematic theology (constructive, philosophical theology)". Those on the other hand who conceived of their work as including one or more additional concerns, such as presuppositional studies ["principles of theology (methodology)"], historical studies ["dogmatics (history of doctrine, symbolics)"], or other interests (the assumption being that some systematic theologians might be involved in an even broader range of subjects, from interaction with the general sciences and the sciences of religion to biblical theology, moral theology, as well as practical, pastoral theology), would be able to check one or more additional categories listed.

We were of course aware that even with this arrangement our choice of terms and selection of categories might still cause difficulties. As we shall see, some difficulties did soon appear.

Our questionnaires were mailed out in several "waves" during the spring and summer of 1974. Cover letters offered a short explanation of the project, referring specifically to the plans for the publication of a DIRECTORY OF SYSTEMATIC THEOLOGY IN NORTH AMERICA, and invited each person who was in any way identified with systematic theology to participate, first by filling out and returning the questionnaire, and secondly by helping us make sure that colleagues who could be considered active participants in the discipline would know about the project and receive a copy of our questionnaire. Responses began to come in immediately, and before long we had some 400 completed questionnaires in our files. Cross-checking our roster, however, we discovered signs of procrastination as well. During the fall and winter of 1974-75 we sent follow-up letters to all those who had not yet responded, and a number of additional questionnaires came in--though by that time we received as many letters indicating non-involvement in systematic theology as completed questionnaires. By the spring of 1975 we had the completed questionnaires from some 580 persons, 560 of which were from bona fide "active professional systematic theologians." We estimated that this represented some 90% of the people involved in the discipline.

The response was most gratifying. Not only did people conscientiously provide the factual information requested; they gave serious and thoughtful attention to the evaluative questions as well. In addition there were many letters from respondents reflecting on the value and importance of the project itself. There were some colleagues, of course, who were not positively inclined when confronted with another questionnaire. One of these wrote, "I can't think of anything the world needs less than a directory of systematic theology; I feel sufficiently compiled, stamped out, listed, numbered, and categorized for one lifetime!" He did not return the questionnaire, and is consequently not included in the DIRECTORY or in the summaries presented below. His attitude, fortunately, was unique. More typical evaluations of the project were those of the following sort and from the following people:

> "I congratulate you on undertaking a much needed task to describe the present state of the discipline of systematic theology."
>
> --Ralph W. Burhoe
> Meadville Theological School
> Chicago

"I am glad you are undertaking this study of systematic theology; I'll look forward to its results."
--Robert T. Handy
Union Theological Seminary
New York

"I am quite interested in your idea of trying to describe and get hold of 'the present state of the discipline of systematic theology', and would be especially interested in the categories for selection, and methodology, which you intend to employ."
--David H. Fisher
School of Theology
University of the South
Tennessee

"Best wishes for what sounds like a valuable project."
--John J. Heaney
Fordham University
New York

"Your project is a good one, and I will be eager to get the DIRECTORY when it is published."
--Kenneth E. Jones
Gulf Coast Bible College,
Texas

"I am very interested in your project. It's an excellent idea. It could provide a good view of where we are and what is to be done. More than in the DIRECTORY, useful as it would be, I am interested in a solid volume (or two?) on 'Systematic Theology Today'."
--Gustave-Pierre Leonard
Writer-Reviewer,
New York

"It looks like something that is very much needed and I eagerly anticipate its results."
--M. Douglas Meeks
Eden Theological Seminary
Missouri

"This will doubtless be a great boon to all of us in the profession and I hope you will get the cooperation you need to complete it."
--Harold H. Oliver
School of Theology
Boston University

"For some time I have been desirous of closer contacts and more communications with others who share a special interest in systematic and philosophical theology. I have also wanted to be better informed regarding societies and associations whose focus is on systematic theology in particular. You are to be commended for the project which you have undertaken and I look forward to the information which will be made available."

--Robert J. Palma
Hope College
Michigan

"I might add that I think the project is a very good idea, and I am happy to see it undertaken. I'll be most interested in the results."

--Robert P. Scharlemann
The University of Iowa

"I am looking forward with much interest to the completion of your study and with you, best success to this important work."

--Hans Schwarz
Lutheran Theological Seminary
Ohio

"I hope that your DIRECTORY and your analyses are successful... I think that one of the great problems of theology today is the lack of communication among theologians about basic issues.

--Terrence W. Tilley
The Church Divinity School
of the Pacific
California

By the time our data gathering was at the most active stage we were beginning to discover the true magnitude of our task. Not only had our original time frame broken down; we were conscious of the need for additional staff and funding as well. We had hoped that by this time the CSR's application to the NEH for the funding of the so-called "inventory project" would have been granted and that our project could have been incorporated as part of that larger undertaking. This had been suggested to us when we first contacted the CSR's Research and Publication Committee with our plan. Late in the summer of 1974 it became clear, however, that the CSR project would not be funded in its original form. The NEH encouraged the Council to submit an application for funds to undertake a feasibility study, preparatory to another major project proposal, which meant a delay of several years for the inventory project itself. Seeing that our project was already well on its way, while the CSR plan was going back to the drawing board, the Research and Publication Committee encouraged us to seek funds independently and to press on with our work as rapidly as possible. We subsequently made inquiries with the NEH concerning the possibility of obtaining separate funding for our project under the so-called "New Research Tools" program, but because of rather severe restrictions in the definition of that program--especially the rather special concept of "research tools" which had become normative for that program--we were not successful. Later applications on behalf of the project were presented by the University of Tennessee at Chattanooga Office of Development and Planning to various private foundations, among them the Lilly Foundation, but these were also unsuccessful. However, the Faculty Research Committee and the University Administration did decide to continue the support of the project, first through 1975 and later through 1976, and with this we decided to continue our work and to scale the project to our means. We had hoped to engage computer specialists to devise the necessary programs for committing our material to electronic memory, recall, and analysis , but this part of the project had to be changed. Analysis and editing would have to be done manually, and the time frame would consequently have to be extended further. Such, unfortunately, are the realities of life in the humanities-- and perhaps especially in religious and theological studies.

Parallel with the mammoth task of data gathering we proceeded to make certain preparations for the second phase of the project, namely categorization and analysis. In particular, the problem of defining and delimiting the discipline of systematic theology continued to bother us, and the problem of producing an overview of the multitude of subject areas involved in the discipline became more pressing as time went on.

As will be recalled, at the point in our questionnaire where we asked respondents to check the general subject areas in which they were teaching, we had chosen to use the following categories:
   a) principles of theology (methodology);
   b) dogmatics (history of doctrine, symbolics);
   c) systematic theology (constructive theology, philosophical theology);
   d) other (specify).
Most respondents seemed comfortable with this scheme, but a number of people remarked that their particular subject areas were not usually categorized in this manner. In fact, as we began to analyze the questionnaires, we found evidence of considerable equivocation in connection with several key terms. "Dogmatics" was for some the technical term for systematic or constructive theology; for others, as in our scheme, it referred to history of doctrine or tradition studies. "Systematic theology", likewise, for some

people, referred to the history of doctrine, while for others, as in our scheme, it had primary reference to constructive theology. "Symbolics", the traditional term for the study of creedal or confessional theology, seemed very vague to many people--some even took the term in a non-technical sense as having reference to the study of religious language, and particularly the subjects of symbols and myths. "Principles of theology" and "philosophical theology," seemed to cause some people problems also. Some took "principles of theology" to refer to the fundamental portions of systematic theology; most, however, were willing to accept our identification of the term with methodological concerns and its location apart from systematic theology proper. "Philosophical theology," on the other hand, tended for many to have connotations different from systematic theology. They apparently considered the term as having reference to philosophical content, not philosophical process, and wanted it separated from systematic theology as such. Finally, most problematic of all, was a term which we had not proposed to use, namely "fundamental theology." Apparently in vogue in wide circles, it carried a wide range of references--all the way from principles of theology and history of doctrine to systematic or constructive, even biblical theology. Professors of "fundamental theology" thus showed considerable disagreement as to what they considered fundamental.

In sorting out these many equivocations, we were convinced that our over-all scheme was defensible, but that the three major categories should be reformulated. We decided that there was strong support for our use of the terms "dogmatics" and "systematic theology" and that we would continue to consider the first as primarily related to history of doctrine and the second as having primary reference to constructive theology. We also decided that "principles of theology" most clearly refer to methodological matters, and that "philosophical theology" is most immediately related to constructive or systematic theology. In the end, therefore, our scheme came to look like this:
   a) theological methodology (principles of theology, prolegomena);
   b) historical theology (history of doctrine, dogmatics);
   c) constructive theology (philosophical theology, systematics);
   d) other.
These are the major categories which we shall operate with below. We subsequently went back over our material and edited the responses to conform to these general categories. In no case, however, did we change any responses; all we have done is to categorize the information according to the above classifications so as to provide a basis for consistent analysis and clear comparisons.

We were next faced with the problem of developing an over-all scheme for the description and analysis of the specific subject areas--the content or subject matter--which theologians are concerned with. A number of questions on our questionnaire included references to specific subjects or subject areas--undergraduate majors, areas of concentration in seminary and graduate schools, dissertation topics, teaching responsibilities, research interests, current research projects, etc. We had not at any point predefined any categories to be used in answering these questions; we wanted each respondent to be free to describe his subject areas or specific topics in his own particular way. Our task now was to draw out all of these descriptions and systematize them in such a way as to allow us to analyze the material within a consistent framework and describe the work going on among systematic theologians in an orderly manner.

The task was exhausting as well as time consuming. The first step was to make a list of every subject or subject area referred to by our respondents. Next we sought to identify the major groups of subjects or subject areas. And finally, there was the task of sorting out the various sub-species of subjects or subject areas within each major group and listing them in a logical order. We tried several different schemes before we finally settled on one that seemed to satisfy us and accommodate all the material. The scheme we settled on included separate divisions for "prolegomena," "general sciences," "sciences of religion," biblical studies," "theological studies," "historical studies," and "practical studies." Within each of these divisions we then sought to list the respective disciplines of study in logical order. Finally within each discipline of study we listed the particular categories of subjects or subject areas which were related to it in logical order. In one discipline, namely systematic theology, it was necessary to develop a separate, more detailed over-view of subjects--an outline of major doctrines and doctrinal subjects, logically arranged. This was added at the end of the scheme. I shall list the over-all scheme here, since it will be basic to the understanding of the analyses to follow:

Subject Areas

Overview

1000 Prolegomena
2000 Sciences (in general)
3000 Sciences of Religion
4000 Biblical Studies
5000 Theological Studies

```
6000   Historical Studies
7000   Practical Studies
8000   Systematic/Dogmatic Subject Areas
```

Categories

1000   Prolegomena

```
1100   Theological Propaedeutic
1110      Nature of Theology
1120      Relationship of Theological Disciplines
1200   Theological Methodology (general)
1210      Presuppositional Studies
1220      Approaches to Theology
1300   Theological Criteriology
1310      Principles of Truth, Norms
1320      Authority
1400   Theological Ecology (Context of Theology)
1500   Theological Ideology (Point of View)
1600   Theological Typology (Classification)
```

2000   Sciences   (in general)

```
2100   Anthropology
2200   Sociology
2300   Psychology
2400   Languages, Literature, Classics
2500   History
2600   Philosophy
2610      Metaphysics
2611         Epistemology
2612         Ontology
2613         Axiology
2614         Aesthetics
2620      Analysis
2621         Logic, Language Theory
2622         Philosophy of History
2623         Philosophy of Science
2624         Philosophy of Law
2700   Natural and Physical Sciences
2800   Political Science
2900   Arts
```

```
2910    Economics, Business Administration
2920    Law
2930    Education
2940    Engineering
2950    Naval Science
```

3000 Sciences of Religion

```
3100  History of Religion, Phenomenology of Religion
3200  Sociology of Religion
3300  Psychology of Religion
3310    Psychology of Death
3400  Philosophy of Religion
3410    Religious Epistemology
3420    Religious Language
3500  Philosophical Theology
3510    Theological Metaphysics (Theistic Studies)
3600  Philosophical Ethics
```

4000 Biblical Studies

```
4100  Biblical Languages
4200  Hermeneutics, Principles of Interpretation
4300  Biblical Criticism (Literary Studies)
4400  Biblical Interpretation (Exegesis)
4500  Biblical Theology
4510    Old Testament
4520    New Testament
4530    Thematic Studies
```

5000 Theological Studies

```
5100  Symbolics (Creedal Theology)
5200  Canonical, Conciliar Theology
5300  Catechetical Theology
5400  Systematic Theology
5410    Introductory Studies (Surveys, Methodology)
5420    Systematic Studies (Constructive, Integrative)
5430    Thematic Studies (cf. 8000 category, below)
5500  Apologetics
5600  Moral Theology, Theological Ethics
```

5610   Personal Ethics
5620   Social Ethics
5630   Ethical Themes
5700 Theology and Science, Theology and Technology
5800 Theology and Culture
5900 Theology and Art, Theology and Literature

6000   Historical Studies

6100 History of Ideas
6110   Classical Period
6120   Medieval Period
6130   Modern Period
6140   Contemporary Period
6200 Church History
6300 History of Doctrine, History of Christian Thought (Dogmatics)
6310   Introductory Studies (Overview, Survey)
6320   Motif Studies (Thematic)
6330   Period Studies (Chronological)
6331   Patristics
6332   Medieval, Scholastic Studies
6333   Reformation Studies
6334   Modern Period
6335   Contemporary Period
6340   Area Studies (Geographic)
6350   Tradition Studies (Denominational)
6360   School Studies (Ideological)
6370   Studies of Individual Theologians
6380   Comparative Studies

7000   Practical Studies

7100 Parish Ministry, Church Administration
7110   Church and Society
7200 Worship, Liturgy, Spiritual Theology
7300 Ministry of the Word
7310   Preaching
7320   Teaching
7330   Evangelism
7340   Missions
7400 Pastoral Theology, Pastoral Care
7500 Ecumenics

7600 Interfaith Dialogue
7700 Church Polity, Church and State
7800 Public Education, Higher Education

8000   Systematic/Dogmatic Subject Areas

8100 Doctrine of Revelation
8110   General Revelation (Nature, History, Reason)
8120   Special Revelation
8130   Scripture
8140   Experience (Tradition, Faith)
8200 Doctrine of God
8210   Being and Nature of God (Trinity, Attributes of God)
8220   Works of God
8230   Creation and Providence
8231   World (Nature, History, Tragedy, Miracles)
8232   Man (Theological Anthropology, Sin, Death)
8240   Election and Covenant
8241   Law and Promise (Will of God)
8250   Redemption and Salvation (Soteriology)
8251   Grace
8300 Doctrine of Christ (Christology)
8310   Person of Christ (Incarnation)
8311   Mariology
8320   Work of Christ (Atonement)
8321   Death and Resurrection
8400 Doctrine of Holy Spirit (Pneumatology)
8410   Nature of Holy Spirit
8420   Gifts of Holy Spirit (Charismatics)
8500 Doctrine of Church (Ecclesiology)
8510   Nature and Mission of Church
8520   Means of Grace (Sacraments)
8530   Membership and Ministry (Apostolicity, Ordination)
8600 Doctrine of Christian Life
8610   Relation to God (Justification, Faith, Devotion, Prayer)
8620   Relation to Others, World (Sanctification, Vocation)
8700 Doctrine of Consummation (Eschatology)
8710   Kingdom of God (Christian Hope)
8720   Judgment

There were, of course, a great many other aspects of our material which required collating, categorizing and summation, as we worked to gain an overview of the active participants in the discipline. Much of this was related to the editing of the individual biographical sketches and the final preparation of the manuscript for the DIRECTORY. This part of the process has been fully described in the introductory chapter of that work.

We were conscious of two specific needs: we wanted to find a format that would allow us to present a great deal of information in a limited amount of space and with a minimum of duplication; yet we wanted to present the material in such a way as to provide an opportunity for quick cross-referencing and easy correlations. This would be of importance both for the usefulness of the DIRECTORY and in preparing the analyses to be included in the present book. By the time we came to undertake the final editing of our material for inclusion in the DIRECTORY, we had therefore decided to utilize a system of numerical values, acronyms, etc., all cross-referenced to indexes containing the keys to each particular category. All the biographical sketches were edited down to a single page and re-typed according to a uniform model. To the left on each page were included the various classifications of information; to the right, the data given in full where possible and necessary, and by way of numerical codes or other symbols where this was possible and permissable. It remains to be seen, of course, whether this format will prove to have fulfilled our needs. It is clear that the individual theologians involved have in some sense been "Compiled, stamped out, listed, numbered, and categorized," just as our lone conscientious objector predicted. But behind the cold numerical values are the actual realities, the individual personalities, flesh and blood, as well as the various corporate contexts, institutions and organizations, all accessible and easily identifiable.

The preparation of the present volume has of course involved additional summarizations and collations. As will be seen, all the analyses included in Part I of this work are based on the material presented in the DIRECTORY. We had hoped that this material could have been computerized and that the necessary collating and correlating could have been done by those quick and capable machines. However, this was not to be. Instead, our staff did this work manually. And this is not all. Part II of this book is based on the multitude of responses we have received to the evaluative questions included in the questionnaire--material not included in the earlier work. No one can imagine the amount of time and effort involved in developing these summary overviews, particularly the process of systematizing and organizing the many different comments--all individual, in perspective as well as style. In order to handle these responsibly, we transferred every individual answer to 3 x 5 cards, organized them according to content, perspective and point of view, and finally determined the relative strength of the various statements by reference to the prevelance of similar opinions.

By the end of 1976, all these tasks had been completed. The manuscript of the DIRECTORY was in the hands of the CSR Research and Publication Committee, and we were finally ready to write our concluding report, THE STATE OF THE ARTS IN NORTH AMERICAN SYSTEMATIC THEOLOGY TODAY.

An outline of the following chapters might be useful at this point. As already stated, Part I of this work is based on the factual information presented in the DIRECTORY; it focuses therefore on the people involved in the discipline of systematic theology at the present time. Chapter I ("Systematic Theologians: A General Profile") summarizes a series of items having to do with personal and professional facts, such as age, place of birth, denominational affiliation, current position, career (past positions, academic as well as non-academic), etc. The chapter is clearly--pardon the expression--the most nuts-and-bolts-oriented of the lot, but I hope that those who desire to know something about the grass-roots of the systematic theological community will bear with it and read through it. It does provide a useful--perhaps even surprising--family portrait of the active practitioners of the art today.

Chapter 2 ("Systematic Theologians: Training and Background") focuses specifically on the educational background and academic qualifications of the people involved in the discipline at the present. It looks at such matters as undergraduate majors, graduate studies, terminal degrees, areas of concentration, dissertation topics, dissertation supervisors, and other items of importance for the understanding of the mindset and orientation of the present generation of systematicians. The material also provides an opportunity to reflect on the quality and direction of the educational processes by which systematic theologians are developed in our time.

Chapter 3 ("Systematic Theologians: The Daily Tasks") analyzes information which bears on the day-to-day teaching responsibilities and professional involvements of people in the discipline. It gives overviews of the range, levels, and general subject areas of the systematicians' teaching; summarizes the specific subjects of courses they offer; and takes a look at the kinds of sources that are most prevalent in their course syllabi. The chapter also includes an analysis of the number of memberships systematic theologians hold in professional societies of various kinds.

Chapter 4 ("Systematic Theologians: Research Interests and Active Projects") concentrates on what might be called the "growing edge" of the discipline of systematic theology: the general research interests which seem to guide the systematicians' work and the active research projects which they are presently involved in. The chapter gives an impression of what we can expect the active professionals in the discipline to produce in the way of publications in the foreseeable future and what the subjects or subject areas are that appear to have the strongest hold on the attention of systematic theologians at the present. As a final section, we have included a complete collation of all the contexts in which we have made analyses of the relative strength of the different major subjects or subject areas in the background, the work and the thought of systematic theologians in North America.

With the conclusion of Chapter 4 (and thereby Part I) we can consider ourselves introduced to the systematic theological community at the present. But as with most introductions, the information summarized says little about "the inner man," the content of the thought, the self-consciousness, the hopes and aspirations of the systematic theologians themselves. This is what Part II, Chapters 5 through 8, is all about. It will be published shortly.

Chapter 5 ("Systematic Theology: A Status Report") presents an analysis of the comments we received in response to the question, "How would you describe the current state of the discipline of systematic theology?" A preliminary summary of this material was presented at the Annual Meeting of the American Academy of Religion in 1975; it was subsequently printed in the proceedings of that meeting ("The Present State of the Discipline of Systematic Theology--A Preliminary Report," PHILOSOPHY OF RELIGION AND THEOLOGY: 1975 PROCEEDINGS, James William McClendon, Jr., ed., AAR, 1975, pp. 43-50). The presentation here will be considerably more detailed and therefore greatly expanded. We shall also include a number of representative quotations, allowing the systematicians to speak for themselves.

Chapter 6 ("Systematic Theology: The Task Ahead") is a summary and analysis of the responses we received to the question, "What in your view is the main task facing systematic theologians in the foreseeable future?" A quick overview of this material was published in THE CHRISTIAN CENTURY, March 17, 1975, pp. 43-50). The presentation here will of course be more extensive, both in scope and in detail. Once more we shall have opportunity to listen to the people involved, as they reflect in their own ways and words about the task ahead.

Chapter 7 ("Systematic Theology: Means and Methods") focuses on the responses to the question, "How would you describe your own theological method?" For the understanding of the systematic theologian at the present, this is perhaps the most crucial chapter. The extensive material will be systematized here in reference to the various major methodological options that emerge, and the different "schools" of thought or affinities of mind will be described in terms of the presuppositions and prerequisities that are set forth by representative voices in each group. Quotations from our respondents will once again be numerous.

Chapter 8 ("Systematic Theology: Emphases and Mentors") is an analysis of the responses we received to the questions, "What are the most important emphases in your work," and "Which of the major systematic theologians in the past do you consider closest to your own position?" In the first context the attempt is made to systematize the material in terms of dominant trends and major concerns, and the respondents themselves are again liberally quoted. In regard to the references to major mentors out of the past, these are summarized in terms of frequency of occurrence and total spread. We shall thus be able to gain an impression both of the breadth and depth of the influence of such mentors among the systematicians of today.

With the outline of our task thus nailed down, we are ready to proceed to its first facet, the general profile of the contemporary systematic theologian.

Chapter 1

Systematic Theologians: A General Profile

I am occasionally asked by people who know me only as a professor "of something" what my field is. When I say that I teach in the Department of Philosophy and Religion and that my primary interest is systematic theology, many seem puzzled. "Religion" they understand--or think they understand. "Philosophy" is a rather vague concept, at best, but people do generally associate it with thinking. But "systematic theology", what in heavens name does that stand for? I have more than once had that question asked on the first tee and, walking up the fairway between the drive and the approach shot, had to give a thumbnail sketch of what systematic theology means--in my view of it, that is! But not even that seems to make things clearer.

Even in circles that are quite familiar with academic disciplines of study and where the phrase itself does not therefore cause any particular difficulties, the discipline is still surrounded with a certain aura of mystery and awe. There is something irenic in the title itself--"professor of systematic theology"--something that calls forth images of authority (or presumption), depth (or incomprehensability), and complexity (or confusion). One has in mind the typical German professor--was it not the Germans that invented the term "systematische Theologie" in the first place?-- entering his classroom and having seated his class and opened his voluminous notebook, starting his lecture with the famous phrase, "Also, als Ich gestern gesagt hat...." Even in this country one still expects systematic theology to be done with a German accent!

But times are changing. I have personally made my share of pilgrimages to sit at the feet of the sages of the discipline, only to discover that lo, they are quite as human and as limited as the rest of us! Karl Barth may have believed that the Word of God comes "sänkrecht vom Oben", but theologians are not so untouched and vertical. Those who got to know a Barth, a Brunner, a Tillich, or an Aulén personally were surprised to find them interested in music, art, politics, wine, song, even women! They were found to have their personal limitations--pride, jealousy, anger, thoughtlessness--much like the rest of the species. They were often found to propound half-baked ideas, pursue theological rabbits, chase intellectual mirages, fight theoretical windmills. And when out of the public view they could sit down with you, smoke a cigar or sip a glass of sherry with you, they were found to be positively delightful humorists and story tellers, able to laugh at human quirks and boo-boos--their own as well as others!

The ultimate leveling--short of death--is the observation, "He puts his pants on one leg at the time like the rest of us." Among theologians, this sort of leveling takes place--less drastically--when one gets to know something about the person--when one observes him at his desk, in his home, at the table with his family. When in addition one gets to learn something about the theologian's background, his early life, his religious upbringing, his education, his teachers, the books that influenced his career--then one begins to discover that theology does not come in the form of sterile divinity; it has very earthy roots and is grown in many kinds of soil.

Systematic theology today is living proof of that. The discipline has been democratized and put in the hands of the people who are ordinary persons. They are individuals, yes, but individuals set in a recognizable context of contemporaneity and locality, with a consciousness of cultural background and with involvements in particular forms of social interaction. And the context is varied; it no longer conforms to any traditional stereo-type. Systematic theology is no longer the exclusive domain of certain senior members of theological faculties or certain authorized ecclesiastical figureheads; it is as often done in colleges and institutes, by lay theolo-gians, women, and blacks, and at the fringes of the ecclesiastical establish-ment. Contemporary systematic theologians are found both inside and out-side the traditional frameworks, and they do their work within or without the perspectives passed down from the masters of the past.

Who are they? Where do they come from? What is their orienta-tion? What do they do? These and other questions are important if we desire to know the state of the discipline at the present time, and they can only be answered if we are willing to inquire broadly among the people involved. Answering such questions requires an overview that can only be reached on the basis of detailed information provided by the individual systematic theologian himself. This is what we have attempted to do here. No such family portrait of the discipline has ever been made before. We do not therefore have the ability of comparing the present with the past-- except perhaps with the stereotypes that have come down to us and the general impressions of individual masters with whose life most people are only vaguely familiar. Such comparisons are interesting. But here we will present our picture of the discipline strictly on the basis of factual infor-mation, and simply for the purpose of showing the profile of contemporary systematic theologians, more or less unretouched. Hopefully, a similar portrait can be done again, say ten years from now--and then perhaps in comparison with our findings here.

Numbers in Summary

In our study of the present state of the discipline of systematic theology we intended to cover all active professional systematic theologians, Protestant and Catholic, in the United States and Canada. This would include all persons who presently teach and/or are engaged in research and publication related to subject areas generally assumed to be part of the discipline's domain. We cannot, of course, at this point claim that our coverage is complete. However, we can claim that our study represents something vastly more that a statistical sample. The DIRECTORY contains biographies of some 560 persons, and our various summaries here are based on approximately the same number of responses. We estimate that this represents 85-90 percent of the active professional participants in the discipline in North America at the present time.

The persons included in our study are all involved in Christian theology. This is because systematic theology is by definition integrally related to the life and faith of the Christian community, and does not cut across the presuppositional barriers between the several world religions. Systematic theologians do, of course, consider the subject of the relationship between the Christian faith and other religions--and this both from the standpoint of the faith itself, as part of the faith, and from the perspective of philosophy of religion, as part of the methodological prolegomena to theology. But systematic theology is a discipline of Christian theology. Our study, therefore, does not include Jewish theology or the work of Zen masters, Hindu gurus, or Muslim scribes.

Of the 560 persons we have identified as active professional systematic theologians, 20 individuals or 3.57% are women. This is of course a rather low percentage, but in view of the fact that only in recent decades have women had the opportunity for ordination and a realistic possibility for employment in ecclesiastical and academic-theological fields, we can consider this figure already significant. The fact is that more and more women are now entering seminaries and graduate programs in theology. Women are assuming an increasingly active role in the professional societies, and they are already asserting themselves at the forefront of theological scholarship. We can look for women to assume a greater and greater role in systematic theology in the decades ahead.

No attempt has been made in our study to identify any racial minority groups--blacks, for example, are not listed as such. We do have information concerning the places of birth and states of origin, and are therefore able to identify the nationalities of the people involved in the discipline. Our summaries below present this information in some detail.

The following sections of this chapter summarize our findings in regard to certain personal and professional matters that contribute to the general profile of those involved in the discipline at the present time. Included here are studies of age distribution , places of birth, denominational affiliations, present positions, years of teaching, years in the present position, number of academic positions, and other full time positions. Where percentages are included, they have been calculated on the basis of the total number of people providing the information requested regarding that particular point. The information is current as of the end of the 1975 academic year.

Age of Systematic Theologians

A study of the age distribution of active systematic theologians in North America reveals a series of interesting facts concerning the people that make up this group. It says a great deal about the state of the discipline as well--both at the present and for the immediate future.

Our information indicates that active systematic theologians span the spectrum from 28 to 75 years of age. These are of course the outside limits. Clearly, one cannot expect anyone younger than 28 to qualify for a professional involvement in the discipline--the education required normally includes 6 years of graduate work (3 years of seminary plus 3 years of doctoral studies), the usual college graduate being 22 or 23 when he launches such a program. On the other hand, the normal age of retirement from active service is 65-67-- though a few individuals do manage to continue in an active role beyond that age.

If for purposes of analysis we consider the normal timespan for professional involvement in the discipline as including the 37 years between 28 and 65 years of age, the mathematical median age of active systematic theologians would be 46.50 years. In actuality we might perhaps expect that the majority of scholars in this particular discipline would be somewhat older than the mathematical median, especially in a period such as ours, when the discipline is supposed to be "floundering," suffering from a "lack of new leadership," or "in the doldrums." Our material, however, does not indicate that any such upward adjustment of the actual average age is taking place. On the contrary, the discipline seems strong and well--even youthful. Recruitment of young scholars into the discipline does not seem to be a problem at all. According to our calculations, the actual average age of all active professional systematic theologians between 28 and 65 years of age is at present 43.54 years--a full 3 years below the mathematical median age of 46.50.

Table 1 (page 31a) provides a graphic view of this situation. Altogether 558 respondents provided us the information requested at this point. Of these only 15 persons (2.69%) were 66 years of age or above. 135 persons (24.19%) were between 51 and 65 years of age; 323 (57.89%) were between 36 and 50; and 85 (15.23%) were under 35 years of age.

A comparison of the individual "classes" (the number of people in each age group) shows that the largest single groups are the classes of 42 year olds and 45 year olds, with the classes of 46 year olds, 44 year olds, and 39 year olds following close after. All the largest classes, in fact, fall within that particular part of the age spectrum which spans the 15 years from 35-50 years of age. The 323 persons included here represent a clear majority of all active systematic theologians at the present.

If for purposes of projection one considers that those systematic theologians who are now between 35 and 50 years of age have a minimum of 15 years of active service ahead of them, it seems safe to say that the discipline of systematic theology is well provided for at least in so far as numbers and continuity of active professional personnel is concerned, and at least for that length of time. Our calculations become no less encouraging when we project the situation five years from now, when those who are now between 61 and 65 have retired and those now between 30 and 34 have reached the 35-50 year bracket. At that time a total of 309 persons, or 55.38% of all the active professionals in the discipline (assuming the total number remains the same), will be between 35 and 50 years of age.

As is evident from Table 1, our calculations indicate that in order to keep the total number of systematic theologians constant, there should be an average of 14.29 persons per age class. It is interesting to note that this figure is consistently superseded in most classes in the 31-50 year old group, while the classes in the 51-65 year old group are consistently smaller than the average class. This is another indication that recruitment of younger people for the discipline is strong.

In sum, the facet of the contemporary profile of the discipline

Table I

Age of Systematic Theologians *
(28–65 years of age)

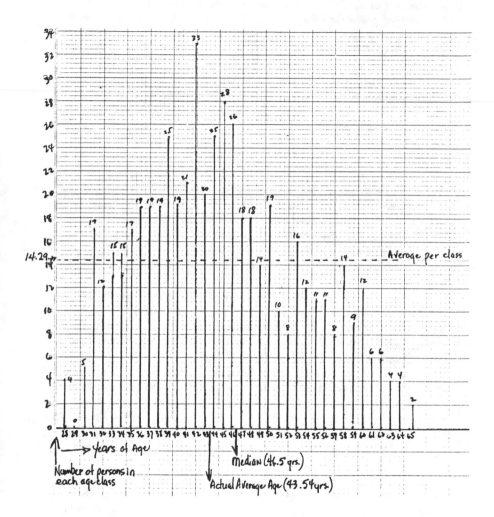

* Total included: 558

which has to do with the age of systematic theologians is very encouraging indeed. The discipline has attracted a great number of younger scholars; recruitment for the future seems to be on a sound footing; continuity of leadership is apparently secured for the next 20 years or more.

Places of Birth

Interesting in the context of our profile of the discipline of systematic theology—though manifestly not integral to the state of the discipline itself—is an inquiry into the places of birth of those presently active as systematic theologians in the United States and Canada.

Of the 555 persons who answered this question on our questionnaire, 480 were born in the United States, 31 in Canada, and 44 in foreign countries. In a discipline which in the past has had the reputation of harboring great numbers of foreigners—one layman volunteered to me even recently that what was wrong with American theology was the domination of German immigrants in the seminaries(!)—we thus find only 7.93% of the active professionals to be born abroad.

An overview of the 44 foreign-born systematic theologians show that 28 come from Western Europe; 9 from Eastern Europe; 6 from Asia; and 1 from Africa. The largest national contingents among Western Europeans are from Germany (7), England (6), and the Netherlands (5); among Eastern Europeans, from Hungary (6) and Czechoslovakia (2); and among Asians, from Japan (3).

Of the 31 Canadian-born systematic theologians on our roster, more than half come from the two provinces of Ontario and Quebec (8 each). Four other provinces, Alberta, British Columbia, New Brunswick, and Saskatchewan, have contributed 3 each.

The 480 American-born systematic theologians we have identified come from 44 different states and the District of Columbia. The majority of these (347 or 72.3%) hail from 16 of the larger states. Table 2 (page 32a) is a graphic overview of the numbers coming from the various states; Table 3 (p. 32 b-c) provides an overview by states and regions, and compares the actual number from each state and region with the relative numbers to be expected, based on population.

As these tables show, all the major sections of the country are well represented in the discipline. The largest contingents, naturally, come

Table 2

Birthplaces of American Systematic Theologians (by States) *

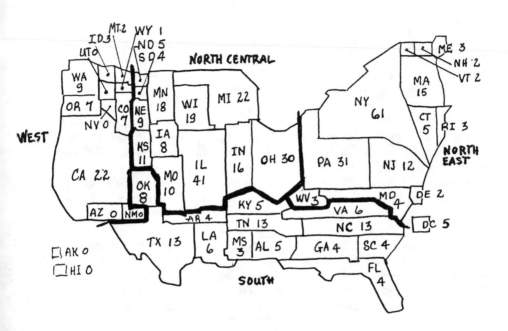

Base map from the Ohio Bureau of Employment Services, copied from
Newsweek, November 15, 1976.
(States are sized according to population.)

* Total included: 480

Table 3

Birthplace of American Systematic Theologians
(by Regions and States, Compared to Population)
(Ranked According to Numbers)

		Actual Number of Systematic Theologians	Number Expected According to Population	Percentage of Actual Total Number	Percentage of Numbers Expected According to Population	Varience
North East:	New York	61	(44.2)	12.7	(9.2)	+3.5%
	Pennsylvania	31	(30.0)			
	Massachusetts	15	(13.7)			
	New Jersey	12	(16.1)			
	Connecticut	5	(6.8)			
	D.C.	5	(2.1)	1.1	(0.4)	+0.7%
	Maryland	4	(8.4)	0.8	(1.75)	-1.0%
	Maine	3	(2.6)			
	Rhode Island	3	(2.8)			
	West Virginia	3	(5.0)	0.6	(1.1)	-0.5%
	Delaware	2	(1.3)			
	New Hampshire	2	(1.8)			
	Vermont	2	(1.1)			
		148	(135.5)	30.9	(28.2)	+2.6%
South:	North Carolina	13	(12.1)			
	Tennessee	13	(9.5)	2.7	(2.0)	+0.7%
	Texas	13	(25.3)	2.7	(5.3)	-2.6%
	Oklahoma	8	(6.3)			
	Louisiana	6	(8.7)			
	Virginia	6	(10.5)			
	Alabama	5	(8.7)			
	Kentucky	5	(8.2)			
	Arkansas	4	(4.7)			
	Florida	4	(13.2)	0.8	(2.9)	-2.0%
	Georgia	4	(10.5)	0.8	(2.2)	-1.4%
	South Carolina	4	(6.3)			
	Mississippi	3	(5.8)			
		88	(129.8)	18.3	(27.0)	-8.7%
North Central:	Illinois	41	(26.6)	8.5	(5.5)	+3.0%
	Ohio	30	(25.8)			
	Michigan	22	(20.8)			
	Wisconsin	19	(10.5)	4.0	(2.2)	+1.8%
	Minnesota	18	(9.2)	3.8	(1.9)	+1.8%
	Indiana	16	(12.4)			
	Kansas	11	(5.8)	2.3	(1.2)	+1.1%
	Missouri	10	(11.6)			
	Nebraska	9	(3.9)	1.9	(0.8)	+1.1%
	Iowa	8	(7.4)			
	North Dakota	5	(1.8)	1.9	(0.8)	+1.1%
	South Dakota	4	(1.8)			
		193	(137.6)	40.2	(28.7)	+11.5%

Table 3 continued

West:	California	22	(41.6)	4.6	(8.7)	-4.1%
	Washington	9	(7.6)			
	Colorado	7	(4.7)			
	Oregon	7	(4.7)			
	Idaho	3	(1.8)			
	Montana	2	(1.8)			
	Wyoming	1	(1.1)			
	Alaska	0	(0.8)			
	Arizona	0	(3.7)			
	Hawaii	0	(1.8)			
	New Mexico	0	(2.6)			
	Nevada	0	(0.8)			
	Utah	0	(2.4)			
		51	(75.4)	10.6	(15.7)	-5.1%

from the North East and North Central states; smaller numbers, expectedly, hail from the Southern and Western regions. The largest single contingent (40.2% of all American-born systematic theologians) comes from the North Central region; the smallest group comes from the West (only 10.6% of our respondents were born in the Western part of the country). The North East has contributed 30.8% of the active professioanls in the discipline; the South, 18.3%. The North Central region has contributed 11.5% more people than would be expected, based on population; the South, 8.7% fewer than could be expected, based on the population of the region. A small over-representation is evident in the figures from the North East region (2.6%); a short-fall of 5.1% relative to population is evident in the figures for the Western part of the country.

An analysis of the actual numbers of systematic theologians compared with the expected relative numbers based on population for each individual state shows that some states have contributed significantly larger contingents that would be expected, while a number of other states are seen to be vastly under-represented. In the NORTH-EAST, the major "over-producers" of systematic theologians are New York (12.7% compared with an expected 9.2%), and the District of Columbia (1.1% compared with an expected 0.4%); "under-producers" are Maryland (0.8% compared with 1.75%) and West Virginia (0.6% compared with 1.1%). In the SOUTH, only Tennessee shows significant over-production (2.7% compared with an expected 2%); major under-producers are Texas (2.7% compared with 5.3%), Florida (0.8% compared with 2.8%), and Georgia (0.8% compared with 2.2%). The NORTH CENTRAL region shows significant over-representation in most states, namely Illinois (8.5% compared with an expected 5.5%), Wisconsin (4.0% compared with 2.2%), Minnesota (3.8% compared with 1.9%), Kansas (2.3% compared with 1.2%), Nebraska (1.9% compared with 0.8%), and the Dakotas (combined 1.9% compared with 0.8%); no states in this region are under-represented in the discipline. In the WESTERN region, a number of states are not represented in the discipline at all, while several states show only a slight over-representation (Washington, Colorado, Oregon, and Idaho); the major factor causing under-representation for the region as a whole is a dramatic short-fall in California (only 4.6% of American-born systematic theologians come from there, compared with an expected 8.7% based on the total population of the state).

Denominational Affiliation

A significant feature in studying the make-up of the community of systematic theologians is the identification of the religious background or denominational affiliation of its members. Not only does this feature help fill in the profile of the discipline at large; it is important for the understanding of the individual systematic theologians as well. It helps explain many significant factors—from general theological orientation to the preoccupation with specific subjects—in the systematic theology of our time.

The 557 persons who answered this particular point in our questionnaire represent some 56 different denominations or religious affiliations. Many of these denominations do, of course, belong within similar or correlative traditions. In fact, of the 56 denominations, 33 are reducible to 13 major denominational "families"; 19 represent minor Protestant denominations and 4 represent "other", Jewish or non-Western orientations.

Table 4 a) and b) (page 34a) give a numerical overview and a graphic sketch of the denominational affiliation of systematic theologians, organized in terms of denominational "families". The first two columns represent a comparison between the number of Roman Catholic systematicians and those with a Protestant affiliation; the last column represents "other" orientations. The middle columns represent the number of systematic theologians in 12 major Protestant church families and the additional category, "other Protestant denominations".

As is clear from this material, the single most strongly represented tradition is the Roman Catholic; 41.5% of all active systematic theologians in North America are members of the Roman Catholic Church. They belong, of course, to a number of orders, rites, societies and congregations, and are thus not an altogether homogeneous group; yet they are undoubtedly more homogeneous than the Protestant group—perhaps even more so than the various Protestant denominational "families" individually.

Of the 57.8% who are Protestant, the largest contingents are the Methodist (18.3% of all Protestant systematic theologians), the Presbyterian (18.0%), the Lutheran (14.3%), the Baptist (12.1%), and the Episcopalian (10.2%). Significant numbers are affiliated with the United Church of Christ (7.5%) and with the Christian Church "family" (4.0%). Table 4 a) gives the percentages for each of these traditions both in relation to all Protestant systematicians and in relation to the total number of systematic theologians on our roster.

The comparison of the percentages of systematic theologians affiliated with various major Protestant denominational families takes on additional significance when these are set in correlation to the membership of these church "families". Table 5 (page 34b) is a graphic presentation of such comparisons for 11 major Protestant denominational "families" in the

34

Table 4 a) and b)

Denominational Affiliation of Systematic Theologians
(By major denominational "families")

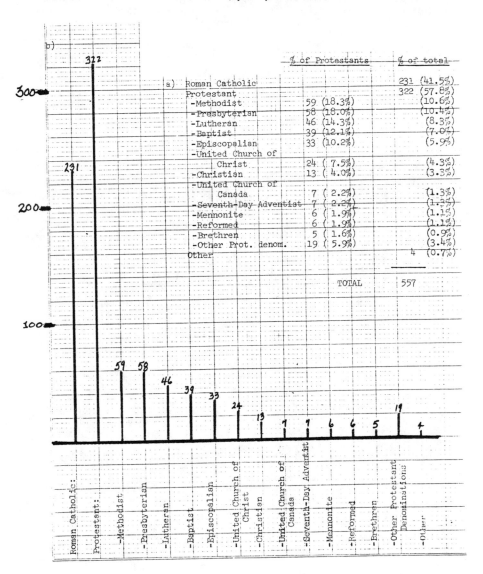

		% of Protestants	% of total
a)	Roman Catholic		231 (41.5%)
	Protestant		322 (57.8%)
	-Methodist	59 (18.3%)	(10.6%)
	-Presbyterian	58 (18.0%)	(10.4%)
	-Lutheran	46 (14.3%)	(8.3%)
	-Baptist	39 (12.1%)	(7.0%)
	-Episcopalian	33 (10.2%)	(5.9%)
	-United Church of Christ	24 (7.5%)	(4.3%)
	-Christian	13 (4.0%)	(3.3%)
	-United Church of Canada	7 (2.2%)	(1.3%)
	-Seventh-Day Adventist	7 (2.2%)	(1.3%)
	-Mennonite	6 (1.9%)	(1.1%)
	-Reformed	6 (1.9%)	(1.1%)
	-Brethren	5 (1.6%)	(0.9%)
	-Other Prot. denom.	19 (5.9%)	(3.4%)
	Other		4 (0.7%)
		TOTAL	557

Table 5

Number of Systematic Theologians in Major US Protestant Denominations
(Comparison by percentages, relative to membership)

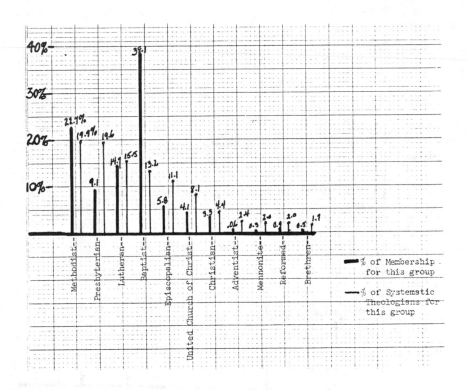

United States. In this table, percentages have been calculated, for purposes of comparison, on the basis of the total membership of the churches in this group (54.5 million) and on the basis of the total number of systematic theologians affiliated with these denominational families (296).

These calculations show that two denominational "families", namely the Baptist and the Methodist, are under-represented in the community of systematic theologians, while several other traditions, notably the Presbyterian, the Episcopalian, and the United Church of Christ, are markedly over-represented. Most dramatic is the short-fall among Baptist. The Baptist "family" comprises an impressive 38.1% of the membership of this group of Protestant denominations; its percentage of the systematic theologians affiliated with these denominational families is a meager 13.2%--all of which adds up to a shortfall of 24.9% or 75 systematic theologians! The Methodist short-fall, in comparison, is small--its membership percentage is 22.7, its percentage of systematic theologians 19.9, making the shortage 2.8% or 8 systematic theologians.

While these calculations prove on the one hand that Baptists and Methodists are less involved in systematic theology than the size of these denominations warrants, they show on the other hand an impressive level of involvement in the discipline among members of the Presbyterian, Episcopalian, and United Church of Christ "families". Each of these traditions has twice as many systematic theologians as is indicated by the numerical strength of their membership--among Presbyterians we find an overplus of 10.5% or 31 systematic theologians; and in the United Church of Christ tradition, 8.1% or 12 systematic theologians. No one will begrudge these denominational "families" their theological strength, of course. It is nevertheless to be regretted that the Baptist and the Methodist traditions do not show the same level of concern for making contributions to the discipline of systematic theology at the present.

Years of Teaching

Our study of the present state of the discipline of systematic theology has included a number of items related to the professional careers of systematic theologians, namely total years of teaching, present position, number of years in the same position (i.e. the same institution), number of academic positions (i.e. mobility), and number and nature of other full-time positions. These inquiries are summarized in the following several sections of this chapter.

35

Altogether 556 persons responded to the question concerning total years of teaching. A number of people included years of teaching on the high school level, but this level of instruction has been edited out of our DIRECTORY and has not been included in our summaries here. Only years of teaching on the college level and above are included in the following calculations.

According to our information, the teaching careers of the active systematic theologians in North America run from 1 to 50 years of duration. If as we have assumed above (page 30), the normal length of an active teaching career in systematic theology is limited to 37 years (from age 28 to age 65), the mathematical median for active careers is 18.5 years. When we calculate the actual average teaching career of those presently active in the discipline, however, we find it to be fully 5 years shorter than the mathematical median, namely 13.51 years. Obviously, although a number of people involved in the discipline have rather long and distinguished teaching careers behind them, the contemporary community of systematic theologians seems on the whole quite youthful and on the average less experienced than could be expected.

The low average total years of teaching for the group as a whole can have several different reasons, of course. Systematic theologians may simply be late in starting their teaching careers, leaving themselves fewer years for active involvement in the discipline. This, however, does not seem to be the case. As we saw above (page 31), the average age of systematic theologians in North America is 43.54 years. When we consider the fact that the same group that has an average age of 43.54 has an average of 13.51 years of teaching behind them, the average systematic theologian is apparently starting his teaching career at the age of 30! The explanation for the comparatively low average years of teaching among contemporary systematic theologians must therefore be found elsewhere--and where better than in the dramatic increase in the number of young, beginning scholars who have become interested in systematic theology and have joined the ranks in recent years? Unfortunately, we have not in our study been able to check the precise correlation of the age and total years of teaching for individual systematic theologians, and we are therefore not in the position to prove whether this correlation of the relative youthfulness of personnel in the discipline and the relative inexperience in teaching actually holds. In general, however, it seems a logically defensible assumption.

Table 6 (page 36a) is a graphic presentation of the information provided us on this point. It represents an overview of the total years of teaching, indicating the number of people in each "class" (the number of persons

Table 6

Total Years of Teaching, Systematic Theologians

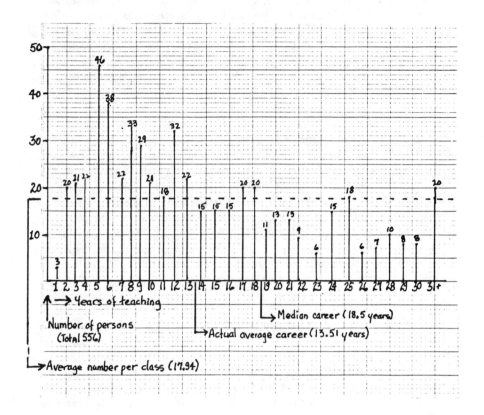

at each stage in a teaching career), and shows the relative inexperience of contemporary systematic theologians quite dramatically. Of the 556 people who responded to this point in the questionnaire, 150 persons or 26.98% had been teaching less than 6 years. In fact, the largest classes across the entire spectrum were those with only 5 and 6 years of teaching behind them (46 persons or 8.27% and 38 persons or 6.83%, respectively). Of the total number included in this study, altogether 357 persons or 64.21% had teaching careers of 15 years or less. Compared with this, the 179 persons or 32.19% who had been teaching for from 16-30 years represent a minority by the quotient of 2. Only 20 persons or 3.60% have had teaching careers in excess of 31 years duration. This explains the low total average for the group as a whole.

A comparative study of the individual classes in the overview may provide a basis for some interesting projections concerning recruitment of systematic theologians as well. On the assumption that most active members of the discipline are holding positions which involve them continually in teaching, we may be warranted in projecting upon the various classes certain correlative time frames, and thus in attempting to identify some overall trends in the recruitment of systematic theologians in recent years. It appears safe, for example, to conclude that those who have taught a total of 10 years or less have joined the community of systematic theologians since 1965. On this basis, then, the graphic presentation in Table 6 may be taken to show that an extraordinary infusion of new blood has taken place in the discipline during the last 12-14 years, particularly between 1968 and 1970--the period of the proverbial "death of God." All the largest classes in the spectrum appear within the range of this time period-- these classes are, in fact, two to three times as large as the groups that have been teaching for longer periods of time; even the average size classes of those who joined the discipline during the last 12-14 years are larger than the peak classes from the 20-year period preceding. Our calculations show that the mathematical average of systematic theologians for all classes is 17.94. Significantly, all the classes with from 2 to 13 years of teaching experience are larger than this average--some even by impressive margins. Only 3 of the classes with longer teaching experience are equal to or larger than the average, namely those that have 17, 18, and 25 years of teaching experience.

If these calculations hold, we are left with the surprising fact that precisely during the period when the discipline of systematic theology seemed most seriously troubled--during the late 60s--it experienced its most dramatic numerical increases. What this means is of course difficult to assess, but that the discipline has been seriously affected by the influx of young theologians who have come out of a period described variously as the most iconoclastic, the most radical, the most creative, and the most open-minded period the discipline has ever been confronted with seems certain. We shall want to keep these perspectives in mind as we investigate the various estimates of the discipline, its present state and future possibilities, below.

Present Position

A study of the present positions of systematic theologians in North America adds several additional details to the profile we are attempting to trace. It provides information concerning the context--the institutional setting--in which systematic theology is done; it allows us to analyze the nature of the positions held by systematic theologians, and particularly to determine whether the positions have a primary or secondary relationship to the discipline; and it enables us to say something about the academic rank distribution of North American systematic theologians at the present. An overview of the current geographic location of those active in the discipline can also be produced.

Looking first at the institutional contexts in which North-American systematic theologians are employed, we find that their present positions are just about evenly divided between graduate-professional contexts--seminaries and theological schools primarily committed to ministerial education, whether church-related, independent, or university-based--on the one hand, and more general undergraduate and graduate-level institutions such as colleges, university graduate schools, etc., on the other. Table 7 (page 38a) is a graphic illustration of this situation. Of the 558 persons who responded to our inquiries at this point, 284 individuals or 50.98% of the total number of systematic theologians in North America hold positions in seminaries and theological schools, while 258 persons or 46.24% hold positions in general college or university contexts. 14 persons or 2.51% of the total number hold positions of another nature--either pastoral, executive, or editorial--outside the academic context altogether.

These facts are all significant in interpreting the present situation of systematic theology in North America. The relative strength of the graduate-professional context is not unexpected. This, after all, is the primary and perhaps most natural location of the professional systematic theologian. One would have expected, in fact, that a larger percentage of those who are active in the discipline would have held positions related to seminaries and theological schools. As our material shows, however, a considerable

38

Table 7

Present Position, Systematic Theologians
I: Types of Contexts

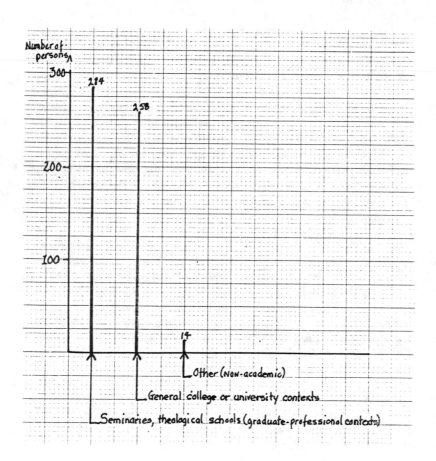

number of systematic theologians hold positions less directly related to the training of ministers and the ongoing life of the church. This may be a matter of necessity--there are only so many positions in the graduate-professional context, and the graduate schools educating systematic theologians may have turned out more candidates for positions during the last 15 or 20 years than the primary market can accommodate. But it may also have to do with the orientation and the sense of professional identity of systematic theologians at the present time. As we shall see shortly, there are signs of a significant broadening of the discipline both in the graduate programs of systematic theologians and in the subject areas which systematic theologians are interested in at the present. Those who are identified with the discipline are thus no longer limited to a narrowly defined subject area, or emerging as specialists who need the particular context that is most conducive to specialization. They are more and more able to function as systematic theologians even in secular contexts--institutions which bring the discipline into interaction with other fields of knowledge, including the sciences in general, the sciences of religion, and other "pre-theological" disciplines. We shall see other signs of these developments below.

Of special interest here is the fact that in North America, only a very small number of people who identify themselves as systematic theologians are active in the pastoral ministry. This may have several different reasons, but the major ones may well be the following two: On the one hand, pastoral work in American church contexts is so time-consuming as to leave systematic theologians employed as clergy little opportunity to nurture any scholarly interests or contribute to the ongoing debate in his discipline; persons who are trained as systematic theologians, but who hold positions as ministers, may therefore be hesitant to claim active participation in the discipline. On the other hand, systematic theology in North America is considered primarily an academic discipline, the prerogative of scholars; thus, just as the church involvements of active ministers tend to work against their participation in the discipline of systematic theology, the academic preoccupations of systematic theologians tend to prevent them from serious interaction with the ongoing ministry of the churches. This situation is an unhealthy one in several respects: The isolation of systematic theologians in institutions of higher education tends to remove the discipline from the actualities of life in the church community, and this is bound to affect the discipline. Also, when the church community itself becomes isolated from scholarly investigation and reinterpretation, this will obviously have an impact on the churches themselves. There are, we should point out, other facets of our material which indicate that the separation between systematic theologians and the ongoing life of the church is not as extensive as is our impression here. We shall return to this point and analyze these matters in more detail below.

Our next concern is to look at the specific positions held by systematic theologians and to determine how many hold positions that are directly related to the discipline and how many hold positions in which systematic theology is only indirectly or secondarily involved. Our approach here is to look at the current titles of those systematic theologians who responded to this point in our study. Many of these titles contain specific references to theology (systematic theology, historical theology, dogmatic theology, fundamental theology, philosophical theology, moral theology, or constructive theology, etc.); many relate more generally to religion (religious studies, philosophy and religion, Bible and religion, etc.); and some provide little or nothing in the way of descriptive references at all. We shall take those titles that have explicit reference to theology to indicate positions that are directly related to the discipline, while those that have no such reference shall be counted as indirectly or secondarily related to the discipline.

Table 8 (page 40a) represents an overview of this material. It shows, first, the number of systematic theologians who hold positions that are directly related to the discipline, and gives a breakdown of the different types of positions involved--whether administrative positions, teaching positions in seminary (the graduate-professional context) or college and university contexts, or dual positions that included both teaching and administrative responsibilities. Also, it includes similar overviews of those whose positions are only secondarily related to systematic theology and those whose positions have not been listed with any descriptive or definitive reference at all.

Several interesting observations can be derived from Table 8. The most obvious is the fact that of the total of 545 systematic theologians who provided the information requested at this point, only 285 persons or 52.29% hold positions that are in some way directly identifiable with the discipline. This means that only a slight majority of professional systematic theologians in North America hold positions which give them an immediate identification as such; there are almost as many systematic theologians who function more or less incognito in positions which are only indirectly related to the discipline. This does not mean that there are only 285 professional systematic theologians in North America--such a narrowing of the profile of the discipline would be entirely unwarranted. It may mean that there are not enough positions with primary focus on systematic theology; but it may also mean that systematic theology has itself become a discipline that relates to and can be pursued in the context of a number of different kinds of positions. We shall look further for signs of such broadening of the discipline below.

Table 8

Present Position, Systematic Theologians
II: Relationship to the Discipline

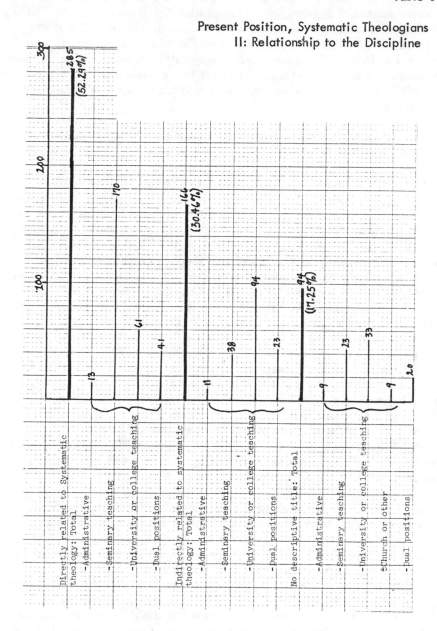

Table 8 also reveals that the single context which provides the greatest number of positions with a direct identification with the discipline of systematic theology is the graduate-professional context. One should not overlook, however, the significant number of such positions found in colleges and universities generally. It may still be the case that systematic theologians find their most natural context in the seminaries and theological schools, but the discipline can obviously find roots and be nurtured in other contexts as well.

One additional item should be noticed here, namely the relatively large number of systematic theologians who hold administrative positions, either full time or in combination with a professional rank. Altogether 117 systematic theologians or 21.47% of our total group hold such positions, ranging from presidents and deans of theological seminaries to directors of campus ministries and directors of continuing education. Considerable numbers serve as department chairmen, either full-time or part-time. It is of course difficult to say whether these figures are unusual in any way, but the impression is unavoidable that systematic theologians seem to have high visibility in positions of academic leadership. Is this once again a sign that systematicians are increasingly recognized as academicians with an inclusive, integrating perspective, and that they are therefore called upon more often than others to give leadership in larger contexts?

When we come to consider the academic rank of North-American systematic theologians at the present, we discover that of the 484 persons who have positions with an identifiable academic rank, the largest single group is that which holds the rank of full professor. However, significant numbers hold the associate and assistant professor ranks. Table 9 (page 41 a) presents this picture graphically. As is shown there, 20 persons or 4.13% of the entire group hold special chairs; 207 persons or 42.77% are full professors; 96 or 19.83%, associate professors; 123 or 25.41%, assistant professors; and 28 or 5.79% are instructors or lecturers.

This picture becomes more interesting when considered in correlation with the average age of systematic theologians and the average total years of teaching calculated above (Tables 1 and 6, pages 31a and 37a, respectively). We found in that connection that systematic theologians have an average age of 43.54 years and have an average teaching career of 13.51 years behind them. If for the sake of comparison we calculate the average rank for persons included in Table 9, we find that it comes to a value of 3.14 on a scale from 1 (instructor) to 5 (special chair), which corresponds to the rank of associate professor with one-sixth of the service normally required for promotion to full professor (i.e. associate professor with one year of service). When we consider that most faculty members with doctor-

41

Table 9

Present Position, Systematic Theologians
III: By Rank

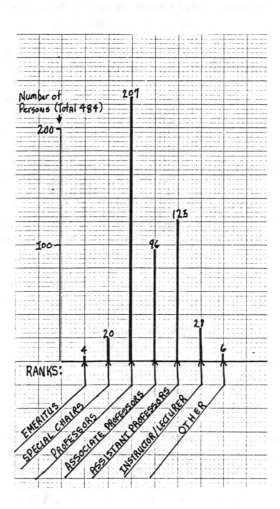

Number of Persons (Total 484)

RANKS: EMERITUS, SPECIAL CHAIRS, PROFESSORS, ASSOCIATE PROFESSORS, ASSISTANT PROFESSORS, INSTRUCTOR/LECTURER, OTHER

ates begin their teaching careers in the rank of assistant professor, and that it normally takes only 6 years of teaching to be promoted to associate professor, we are struck by the fact that the average rank for the group as a whole seems rather low. As we said, systematic theologians have an average of 13.51 years behind them; why does it take them this long to obtain the service required in that rank for promotion to full professors?

The answer seems obvious: Either systematic theologians stay in the rank of assistant professors for an unusually long period of time, or they have to serve as associate professors longer than normal before finally being promoted to full professors. We shall not be able to verify which of these alternatives is the case--we did not in our questionnaires ask specifically about years of service in each rank. Whatever the case, however, it seems safe to say that systematic theologians appear to have to serve, like Jacob, a double season for their Rachel! Although there are significant numbers of people who have reached the highest rank, many appear to have to stand in line for longer than normal periods before attaining to that stage of academic prominence and maturity.

One final aspect of our survey of the present positions of systematic theologians in North America must be presented at this point: an overview of their geographic distribution. Of the 557 persons whom we have included here, 46 or 8.26% are located in Canada. The majority of these, namely 23, are in the province of Ontario; the second largest contingent, namely 12, is located in Quebec. Smaller numbers are working in Alberta (4), and in Nova Scotia (3); only the provinces of British Columbia and Prince Edward Island have no systematic theologians at all.

The 511 systematic theologians who are located in the United States and its territories are distributed over 39 states plus the District of Columbia and Puerto Rico; 11 states apparently have no professional systematic theologians at all. Table 10 (page 42a) represents a graphic overview of the distribution of American systematic theologians; Table 11 (page 42b) provides an overview by states and regions, and compares the actual number located in each state and region with the relative numbers that would be expected in each case, based on population.

These tables show that systematic theologians are at work in all major regions of the country, and that the two largest contingents, expectedly, are in the North Central and North East regions. The largest single contingent is in the North Central region; 201 systematic theologians or 39.3% of the total number identified are working in that region. This represents a considerable over-plus relative to the population of the region; in fact, based on population, the North Central region would be expected to

Table 10

Present Location of American Systematic Theologians (by States)

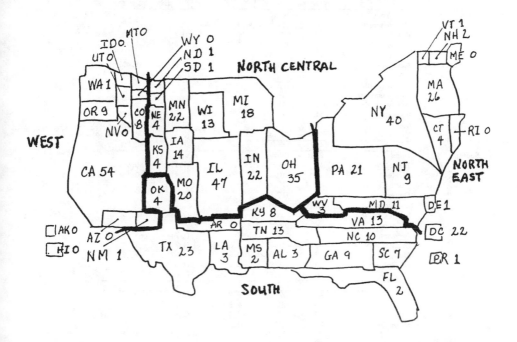

VT 1
NH 2
MTO
IDO. ME O
UTO WY 0
ND 1 MA
SD 1 NORTH CENTRAL 26
WA 1
NY
OR 9 MN MI 40 CT RI 0
CO NE 22 WI 18 4
NVo 8 4 13
WEST NORTH
CA 54 IA IN EAST
KS 14 IL 22 OH PA 21 NJ
4 47 35 9
OK MO
4 20 WV MD 11 DE 1
AKO KY 8 3
AZ 0 AR 0 VA 13 DC 22
RIO TN 13 NC 10
NM 1 TX 23 LA MS AL 3 GA 9 SC 7 PR 1
3 2
FL
SOUTH 2

Base map from the Ohio Bureau of Employment Services, copied from
Newsweek, November 15, 1976.
(States are sized according to population.)

Table 11
Present Location of U.S. Systematic Theologians
(Ranked According to Numbers by Regions and States)

		Actual Number of Systematic Theologians	Number Expected According to Population	Percentage of Actual Total Number	Percentage of Number Expected According to Population	Varience
North East:	New York	40	(45.4)			
	Massachusetts	26	(14.1)	5.1	(2.8)	+2.3%
	D.C.	22	(2.2)	4.3	(0.4)	+3.9%
	Pennsylvania	21	(30.8)	4.1	(6.0)	-1.9%
	Maryland	11	(8.6)			
	New Jersey	9	(16.4)	1.8	(3.2)	-1.4%
	Connecticut	4	(7.0)	0.8	(1.4	-0.6%
	West Virginia	3	(5.1)			
	New Hampshire	2	(1.9)			
	Delaware	1	(1.4)			
	Vermont	1	(1.1)			
	Maine	0	(2.7)		(0.5)	-0.5%
	Rhode Island	0	(2.4)		(0.5)	-0.5%
		140	(139.1)	27.4	(27.2)	+0.2%
South:	Texas	23	(25.9)			
	Tennessee	13	(9.7)	2.5	(1.9)	+0.6%
	Virginia	13	(10.8)	2.5	(2.1)	+0.4%
	North Carolina	10	(12.4)			
	Georgia	9	(10.8)			
	Kentucky	8	(8.4)			
	South Carolina	7	(6.5)	1.4	(1.3)	+0.1%
	Oklahoma	4	(6.5)			
	Alabama	3	(8.9)	0.6	(1.7)	-1.1%
	Louisiana	3	(8.9)	0.6	(1.7)	-1.1%
	Florida	2	(13.5)	0.4	(2.6)	-2.2%
	Mississippi	2	(5.9)	0.4	(1.6)	-1.2%
	Arkansas	0	(4.7)		(0.9)	-0.9%
		97	(132.9)	19.0	(26.0)	-7.0%
North Central:	Illinois	47	(27.3)	9.2	(5.3)	+3.9%
	Ohio	35	(26.5)	6.8	(5.2)	+1.6%
	Indiana	22	(12.7)	4.3	(2.5)	+1.8%
	Minnesota	22	(9.5)	4.3	(1.9)	+2.4%
	Missouri	20	(11.9)	3.9	(2.3)	+1.6%
	Michigan	18	(21.4)			
	Iowa	14	(7.6)	2.7	(1.5)	+1.2%
	Wisconsin	13	(10.8)			
	Kansas	4	(5.9)			
	Nebraska	4	(4.1)			
	North Dakota	1	(1.9)			
	South Dakota	1	(1.9)			
		201	(141.5)	39.3	(27.7)	+11.6%
West:	California	54	(42.7)	10.6	(8.4)·	+2.2%
	Oregon	9	(4.9)	1.8	(1.0)	+0.8%
	Colorado	8	(4.9)	1.6	(1.0)	+0.6%
	New Mexico	1	(2.7)			
	Washington	1	(7.8)	0.2	(1.5)	-1.3%
	Alaska	0	(0.8)			
	Arizona	0	(3.8)		(0.7)	-0.7%
	Hawaii	0	(1.9)			
	Idaho	0	(1.9)			
	Montana	0	(1.9)			
	Nevada	0	(0.8)			
	Utah	0	(2.4)		(0.5)	-0.5%
	Wyoming	0	(1.1)			
		73	(77.6)	14.3	(15.2)	-0.9%

42b

have 142 systematic theologians or 27.7% of the total group. Its over-plus
is thus the equivalent of 11.6%. The region with the largest short-fall of
systematic theologians is the South; 97 systematic theologians or 19% of
our group are at work there. Based on population, the South should have
some 133 systematic theologians or 26% of the group; the short-fall, then,
is the equivalent of 7%.

     An analysis of the relationship between the actual number of system-
atic theologians and the expected number relative to population for each
individual state shows that a number of states employ considerably higher
numbers of systematic theologians than would be expected, while a number
of other states do not have as many positions in the discipline as could be
expected. In the NORTH EAST region, the District of Columbia and Mass-
achusetts employ more systematic theologians than the expected average by
population (3.9% and 2.3% respectively); several states in this region employ fewer systematic theologians than warranted by population, among
them, Pennsylvania, New Jersey, and Connecticut. The region as a whole
has just about the number expected relative to population. In the SOUTH,
only three states employ slightly higher numbers of systematic theologians
than expected on the basis of population, namely Tennessee, Virginia, and
South Carolina. All other states in the region show short-falls by percen-
ages of from 2.2 to a fraction of a point, the largest short-fall being in
Florida (2.2%). In the NORTH CENTRAL region, practically every state
shows a higher number of systematic theologians than expected on the basis
of population. The major "over-employers" are Illinois (3.9%), Minnesota
(2.4%), Indiana (1.8%), Ohio (1.6%), and Missouri (1.6%). A few states
fall short of the expected numbers, but only by fractions of a percentage
point. In the WESTERN region, the majority of the states apparently do not
have systematic theologians at all, but the short-fall for the region as a
whole is only slight, due to the fact that California, Oregon and Colorado
employ more systematic theologians than expected by reference to popula-
tion--California by a total of 2.2%.

Years in Present Position

     We shall proceed next to take a quick look at the information we
have gathered concerning the length of tenure (at whatever level) in the
present position (i.e. in the same institution) for systematic theologians in
North America. This material is significant in that it fills in some crucial
details in our profile of the discipline--features which have to do with the
mobility or relative stability of the community of systematic theologians at
the present time. Table 12 (page 43a) is a graphic presentation of this
material.

43

Table 12

Years in Present Position, Systematic Theologians

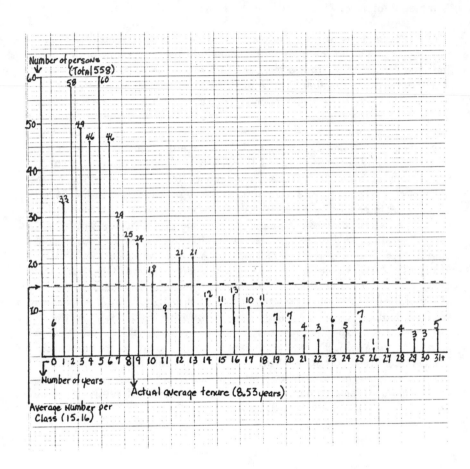

Of the 558 persons who provided answers to this point in our questionnaire, a total of 298 or 53.41% were found to have held their present positions less than 6 years. In fact, all the largest classes in this table appear within that part of the spectrum which refers to length of tenures in the present position of from 2 to 6 years!

Initially, such considerations would seem to indicate that systematic theologians are a restless group and that the discipline is characterized by a high degree of mobility. What we have already said concerning the comparative youthfulness of professionals in the discipline and the low average years of teaching for the group as a whole would seem to undergird this impression of instability and reinforce the expectation of a high degree of mobility in the discipline. Our material, however, does not support such conclusions. On the contrary, when the average years of tenure in the present position is calculated for the entire group of active systematic theologians in North America at the present, the figure proves to be a surprisingly high 8.53 years!

A further glance at Table 12 will serve to explain this remarkable fact. As the overview shows, the classes with from 7 to 13 years in the present position are all except one well above the average for all classes, and the classes with from 14 to 18 years of tenure are all only slightly below the average for all classes. There are, in other words, considerable numbers of systematic theologians with long and faithful service in their present positions. This, of course, is reflected in the over-all average.

Our surprise at finding that systematic theologians have spent an average of 8.53 years in their present position is increased, however, when we consider a) that the same group has been calculated to have an average total years of teaching of only 13.51 years (Table 6, page 37a above), and b) that a total of 26.98% of all systematic theologians have had less than 6 years of involvement in the teaching profession altogether (cf. above, page 37a). The first of these facts means that, on the average, systematic theologians have spent 63.14% of their total teaching careers in their present positions; the second means that half of the people who have a tenure of 6 years or less in their present position have joined the discipline during that span of time and must therefore be considered part of the growth pattern within the discipline and not necessarily as contributing to the restlessness and mobility of the group as a whole. All in all, our inquiry shows that contemporary systematic theologians are a remarkably stable group, professionally. We shall find this impression strengthened further when we come to analyze, next, the information that has come our way concerning the number of positions systematic theologians have individually held during their careers.

44

Our inquiry on this subject was motivated by the desire to know
as precisely as possible the degree of mobility which exists among contemporary systematic theologians. Such information is useful in several
contexts. Not only does it help to make the general profile of the discipline clearer in detail; it may serve the individual theologian as a general yardstick by which to measure his own particular experience and as
a model for predicting--at least hypothetically--what the shape of an average career in the discipline can be expected to be. It may allow us to
compare the mobility of systematic theologians with that of professionals
in other disciplines, as well.

Altogether 555 persons have provided us the necessary information
on this point. The material is set forth graphically in Table 13 (page 45a).
As this table shows, a total of 199 persons or 35.86% of all active systematic theologians in North America have held only one academic position
during their career; 180 persons or 32.43% have held 2 positions; 100 persons or 18.02% have held 3. The classes that have held 5 or more different
positions during their teaching careers are quite small.

Of special interest in this context is the group of people that have
held only one academic position during their career. An overview of the
actual length of tenure for all members of this group is presented in Table
14 (page 45b). As indicated earlier, this group represents a little more than
1/3 of all the people presently active in the discipline. As our inquiry
shows, all the largest classes are--expectedly--on the low side of the spectrum, i.e. with from 2 to 6 years of tenure. One would have expected,
therefore, that the group as a whole would prove to have a comparatively
low average length of tenure, and that the explanation for the fact that a
comparatively high percentage of systematic theologians have held only one
academic position during their career is that a large number of them are
rather young and inexperienced scholars. Our material, however, invali-
dates any such conclusions. As Table 14 shows, there are several larger
than average classes in the middle range of the spectrum as well, i.e.
among those with from 7 to 13 years of tenure. In fact, when the average
length of tenure for the whole group is calculated, it comes to 9.47 years,
which is almost a full year higher than the average number of years in the
present position for all systematic theologians considered altogether.

When the average number of academic positions is calcualted for
all systematic theologians as a group it comes to 2.17. If we hold this to-

Table 13

Number of Academic Positions, Systematic Theologians

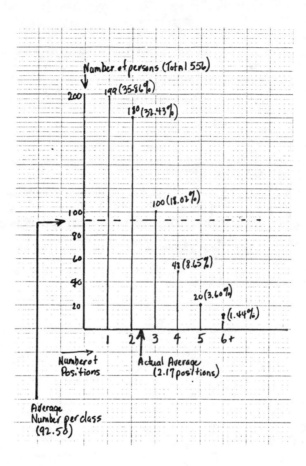

Number of persons (Total 556)

200   199 (35.86%)

180 (32.43%)

100 (18.02%)

100
80
60   48 (8.65%)
40
20   20 (3.60%)
        8 (1.44%)

1   2   3   4   5   6+

Number of
Positions

Actual Average
(2.17 positions)

Average
Number per class
(92.56)

Table 14

Length of Tenure, Systematic Theologians With a Single-Position Academic Career

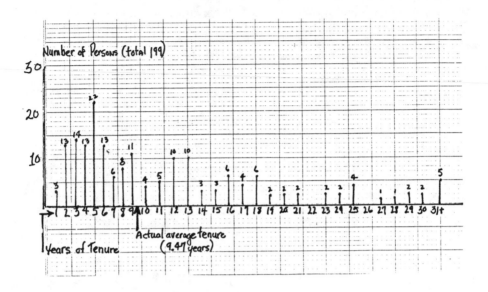

Number of Persons (total 199)

Actual average tenure (9.47 years)

Years of Tenure

gether with the average total years of teaching and the average number of years in the present position calculated above (cf. Tables 6 and 12, pages 37a and 43a), we find the following interesting situation: Systematic theologians who as a group have an average of 13.51 total years of teaching have during that time-span held an average of 2.17 different academic positions, but they have held their present position an average of 8.53 years. Apparently, although systematic theologians may go through a shake-down period early in their career, involving on the average a little more than one move, once they find their place they seem to be a remarkably stable group, settling down to comparatively lengthy tenures.

We ought, perhaps to consider this fact in the light of the larger academic situation also. The mobility of scholars is of course affected not only by personal or internal factors, but by external or social--even economic--factors as well. The job market for academicians, particularly humanists, and especially theologians, has undoubtedly been rather "tight" in recent years. From this perspective, the comparatively long average tenure in the present position (what we have described as the stability of the discipline), and the comparatively low average number of positions held by systematic theologians (low mobility), may in fact reflect negatively on the job situation of the scholars involved. These calculations may actually signify that systematic theologians have less opportunity to move than other scholars, and that the relative stability of the people in the discipline represents a virtue of necessity--even a sign of professional frustration.

Whichever way one interprets these facts, the situation is clear: Systematic theologians do not move often, and when they do they stay in their positions for relatively long periods of time.

Other Full-Time Positions

One final aspect of our inquiries into the professional careers of systematic theologians remains to be summarized here, namely the number and character of whatever other--non-teaching--full-time positions they may have held at various times. Tables 15 and 16 (pages 46a and b) summarize these items.

557 persons provided the information requested on this point. Of these, 287 persons or 51.53% reported no full-time positions outside of teaching; the rest, 270 persons or 38.42% of all systematic theologians surveyed, reported having held a single such "other" position; 53 persons or

Table 15

Number of Other Full-Time Positions, Systematic Theologians

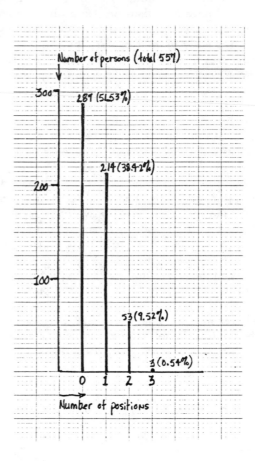

Number of persons (total 557)

300

289 (51.53%)

214 (38.42%)

200

100

53 (9.52%)

3 (0.54%)

0   1   2   3

Number of positions

Table 16

Other Full-Time Positions, Systematic Theologians
(By Categories)

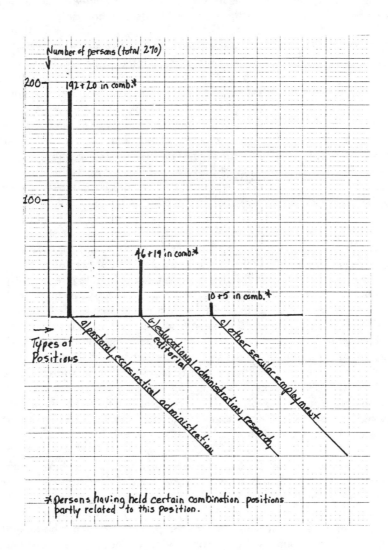

Number of persons (total 270)

200 — 192 + 20 in comb.*

100 —

46 + 19 in comb.*

10 + 5 in comb.*

Types of
Positions

a) pastoral, ecclesiastical administration

b) educational administration, editorial

c) other secular employment

* Persons having held certain combination positions
partly related to this position.

9.52% of the total having held 2; and 3 persons or 0.54% having held 3 or 4. Over-all, our material indicates that systematic theologians are not uniformly and overwhelmingly ivory tower people. Stereotype images of theologians as altogether isolated from the world outside the academy are simply that--stereotypes. Real-life systematic theologians--or at least approximately half of them--do have both contact with and experience from the world outside the hallowed halls of scholarship.

In studying the type of positions which were reported by the 270 persons who have had full-time involvements other than teaching, we found them falling generally into three general categories: a) pastoral ministry and various types of ecclesiastical administration; b) educational administration, research and editorial work; and c) other secular employment. Table 16 is a graphic presentation of the comparative numbers of systematic theologians having held full-time positions of these various kinds. Altogether 212 people or 38.06% of all systematic theologians have been employed in one form or another of pastoral ministry or ecclesiastical administration, research or editorial work; and 15 persons or 2.69% of systematic theologians have held other secular employment.

Of particular interest here is the relatively high percentage of systematic theologians who have had an active involvement for shorter or longer periods in pastoral ministry or in ecclesiastical administration. The point is often made that theology--and systematic theology especially--belongs within the ongoing life of the church, and that systematic theologians ought not to do their work in isolation from the church and with detachment in relation to its ministry. The prevailing impression has been that systematic theologians in recent decades have lost both the understanding of the needs of the church and the desire to speak meaningfully to the people of the church. The trend, we have heard, is toward the secularization of theology; it has been accepted as an unquestioned fact that the interests of theologians go in the direction of the world rather than the church and that they tend to identify with the mind-set of modern men rather than with the commitments and faith of the Christian community.

The fact that 38.06% of all systematic theologians have at one time or another held full-time positions in some form of Christian ministry will hardly satisfy the critics, of course. To many of them, going into a teaching position means leaving the ministry, and they will not be satisfied until the academicians recant and return to the parish. It cannot be denied, however, that the figure is significant. Anyone who has ever held the responsibilities of ministry and administration in the church will have been sensitized to the needs of the church and become aware of what it takes to make theology make sense to church people. Such a background is bound to affect the theologian's work, even in the academy. As we shall see below, this sensitivity to and identification with the ongoing ministry of the church continues to be felt among systematic theologians--is even experiencing a renaissance in this age of secularization--at least in the sense of an uneasy conscience concerning the relationship to the church.

Chapter 2

Systematic Theologians: Training and Background

One of the charms of teaching in an undergraduate setting is the disarming naivite of students who here perhaps for the first time in their life have a chance to come in contact with great ideas--those of the past and those in the making--and get to know scholars who seem able to explain the past and make contributions to the future. Knowledge is something undergraduate students respect with innocence. During their earlier years of schooling they have most often encountered it secondhand--in the form of textbooks and source materials that are utilized by teachers but seldom actually produced by them. Now they suddenly find themselves confronted by scholars who appear as authorities in their field, who write books and make contributions to scholarly journals, who engage in research and read papers at professional meetings, and who are never shy about their own contributions to their discipline. Knowledge is here incarnated before their very eyes; it takes on flesh and blood, reality and contemporaneity--even personality and presence. No one admires a knowledgeable teacher like an undergraduate student, and no one is as prone to choose teachers as models and to dream of college teaching as a career as these young and impressionable disciples.

The undergraduate's enthusiasm usually cools considerably when he discovers what all is involved in becoming a college professor. He has not known of the years of preparation, tight admission standards, high cost, scholarship shortages, prelims, dissertation committees, job hunting, interviews, MBO, publish or perish, tenure committees--he has his mind set on becoming the next Hemingway, a future Freud, a new Einstein, or a second Schweitzer, and now he discovers that in all such and similar fields he cannot expect to get anywhere by way of smart shortcuts and quick improvisation. He must work his way in and up, prove himself at every turn.

The undergraduate who is able to look at these realities and still retain his dreams is a rarity. But a few do persist and somehow manage to work their way through the long and dreary process of preparation--only to discover that the world is still not ready to acknowledge their greatness. Even with a Ph.D. degree in hand, they find that they are not immediately accepted as the leading lights in their discipline. Stuck in a junior position, in a second or third-degree college somewhere, they learn that they are still to be tested, tried. They are not allowed to concentrate in the subject area of their choice. They are overwhelmed with teaching loads and committee responsibilities; underpaid, yet expected to keep a certain image; anxious to prove themselves by way of papers and publications, but finding for the most part that professional meetings proclaim few heroes and that editors permit fewer still to exist.

How does one become a leading light? What does one do to become an authority in one's field? How does one even get to be a knowledgeable member of an academic discipline? Or--the most immediate concern of all professors--how does one become a respected teacher, able to inspire young minds and lead the next generation of scholars to the wellsprings of knowledge?

It is of course impossible to answer such questions specifically, definitely, and authoritatively. Only on the basis of the actual experience of people can one even approximate a sound general judgment. And experience varies--no two persons go through life by exactly the same road. One must therefore make very broad inquiries among the people involved in a certain field. One must consider the great and the mediocre--the fresh brooms and the old foxes. One must summarize, analyze, and compare. And when all is done, one must still guard one's impressions against the temptation of the finite to claim absoluteness.

"How does one become a systematic theologian?" One of my students made a special trip to my office recently to ask that question. My answer at that point, I must confess, was couched in terms of my own experience, with generalizations projected on a larger screen on the basis of my own particular microfiche--I answered him, in fact, as if his question had been, "How did you become a systematic theologian?" I was aware, however, that the original question needed a broader based answer, and knowing that I was going to work on this question in this present book, I promised to let him see the relevant chapter as soon as I finished it.

The answer that I am setting forth here is based on very broad inquiries among contemporary systematic theologians. It summarizes, in fact, a number of items in the biographical sketches of the 560 persons who have responded to our questionnaire and who are included in the DIRECTORY OF SYSTEMATIC THEOLOGIANS IN NORTH AMERICA, namely items that have to do with their education and academic preparation. The various sections of the chapter focus on such details as undergraduate schools, undergraduate majors, seminaries, seminary concentrations, graduate schools, terminal degrees, areas of concentration, dissertation topics, and dissertation supervisors. Our summaries of this material not only enable us to draw in some additional lines in the general composite picture of contemporary systematic theologians which we are trying to develop; it allows us also to identify the institutions and individuals that seem to have had the greatest influence on the present generation of systematic theologians and to make some general observations concerning the educational processes through which these systematicians have come. All in all, the chapter may well represent the broadest possible empirical answer to the question, "How does one become a systematic theologian?"

Undergraduate Schools

The DIRECTORY contains a complete list of the undergraduate schools attended by the currently active professional systematic theologians in North America--397 schools in all. They range from Allegheny College to Yale University; they include "gymnasiums", "seminaries", "scholasticae", state schools, church schools, and private institutions; and they are located in most states in the U.S., in most provinces of Canada, and in 15 foreign countries (Belgium, China, England, Finland, France, Germany, Hungary, India, Italy [Vatican], Japan, Netherlands, Norway, Sweden, Switzerland, and Yugoslavia). The list reads like a random sample of major universities and minor colleges; it includes both leading institutions and unaccredited schools--and gives no ground at all for any solid judgment as to the most appropriate undergraduate starting-point for systematic theologians.

A closer scrutiny of the biographical materials does show, however, that although most of these schools have contributed only one or two graduates to the discipline, there are a number of schools that have been attended by from 3 to 9 persons who are now active in systematic theology. We are able, therefore, to identify and list a certain group of undergraduate schools that have contributed more than most to this particular discipline. The numbers are as follows:

2 schools have contributed 9 graduates
2 schools have contributed 8 graduates
4 schools have contributed 7 graduates
3 schools have contributed 6 graduates
5 schools have contributed 5 graduates
7 schools have contributed 4 graduates
19 schools have contributed 3 graduates
68 schools have contributed 2 graduates
267 schools have contributed 1 graduate

Table 17 (page 53a) lists the names of the schools that have more than 3 graduates represented in systematic theology at the present. The most interesting aspect of this overview is perhaps the fact that certain relatively small private and denominational colleges appear along with the larger universities listed--and ranking high, no less, on the list. For example, Davidson College, a small Presbyterian school, ranks with some of the larger Roman Catholic Universities in the country; and St. Meinrad College, a small Roman Catholic school, has as many graduates in systematic theology as does Yale University.

Denominational schools are on the whole well represented on the list. Baylor University, a Baptist school, is listed with four graduates in the discipline; Ouchita Baptist University and Wake Forest University, another Baptist institution, each have three. Macalester College, a Presbyterian school, adds three to Davidson's seven in the Presbyterian column. St. Olaf College, a Lutheran school, is listed with three graduates among contemporary systematic theologians, and so are Indiana Central College and Ohio Wesleyan University, two Methodist-related schools.

Graduates of the three major independent universities, Harvard, Princeton, and Yale, are of course also well represented among systematic theologians. Finally, smaller but still significant numbers come from other independents such as the College of Wooster, Duke University, University of Chicago, and Vanderbilt University. The only state schools listed as contributing 3 or more graduates to the discipline are the University of Toronto, University of California at Los Angeles, University of Minnesota, and University of Pittsburgh.

The predominance of Roman Catholic institutions on this list is of course related to the fact that by far the largest single denominational group among systematic theologians is the Roman Catholic, and Roman Catholics do normally attend schools that are related to the church and under the direction of church authorities--they do not tend to disperse over such a wide and varied spectrum of educational institutions as Protestants do, and particularly not the students who are preparing for ordination and subsequent graduate work leading to teaching positions. As one can expect, then, a number of major Roman Catholic institutions of higher education such as St. Louis University, Boston College, University of Notre Dame, Fordham University, Loyola University, St. Bonaventure University and Catholic University of America are found listed among the schools contributing comparatively large numbers of graduates to the discipline of systematic theology; in fact, of the 231 Roman Catholics presently active in the discipline, 91 or 39.39% have attended the 17 Roman Catholic institutions included in this particular list.

Table 17

Undergraduate Schools, Number of Graduates in Systematic Theology

Ranking	Number of Graduates		Independent	Denominational (Protestant)	Roman Catholic	State
1.	9	Harvard Universtiy	x			
		St. Louis University			x	
3.	8	Boston College			x	
		University of Notre Dame			x	
5.	7	Davidson College		x		
		Fordham University			x	
		Loyola University (Chicago)			x	
		St. Bonaventure University			x	
		University of Toronto				x
10.	6	Catholic University of America			x	
		Gonzaga University			x	
		Princeton University	x			
13.	5	St. Meinrad College			x	
		Wheaton College (Ill.)	x			
		Wheaton College (Ma.)	x			
		Xavier University			x	
		Yale University	x			
18.	4	Baylor University		x		
		College of Wooster	x			
		John Carroll University			x	
		St. Mary of the Lake Seminary			x	
		University of California (L.A.)				x
		University of Minnesota				x
24.	3	Augustana College		x		
		Borromeo College of Ohio			x	
		College of St. Ignatius (Montreal)			x	
		Duke University	x			
		Hope College	x			
		Indiana Central College		x		
		Loras College			x	
		Macalester College		x		
		Occidental College	x			
		Ohio Wesleyan University		x		
		Ouchita Baptist University		x		
		Providence College			x	
		St. Olaf College		x		
		University of Chicago	x			
		University of Dayton			x	
		University of Pittsburg				x
		Vanderbilt University	x			
		Wake Forest University		x		

A quick look at the undergraduate majors of North-American systematic theologians is useful at this point—if only as a general indication of the "tracks" from which they have come on to the main line of the discipline. Table 18 (page 54a) presents an overview of the information we have gathered on this point, first by general areas or groups of disciplines, then by specific subjects, subject areas or disciplines. In both parts of the overview the various code levels and subject codes are ranked according to the number of people majoring in each, either singularly or in combination with other subjects or subject areas.

As Table 18, Part I indicates, the vast majority of people now involved in systematic theology chose undergraduate majors in the "Sciences in General" (code level 2000); a small minority reports majors in the "Sciences of Religion" (code level 3000); and a few people had undergraduate majors in "Biblical Studies" (code level 4000), "Theological Studies" (code level 5000), and "Historical Studies" (code level 6000). The "Sciences in General" category includes of course, the traditional "arts and sciences"—i.e. both the humanities and the natural sciences. Part II of Table 18 provides a breakdown of the most commonly chosen individual disciplines, all of which are sub-categories of the "Sciences in General".

Among the disciplines of the arts and sciences, "Philosophy" (code 2600) is by far the most common undergraduate major of systematic theologians. Second ranking goes to "Languages, Literature" (code 2400); third, "History" (code 2500); fourth, "Natural and Physical Science" (code 2700); fifth, "Psychology" (code 2300); sixth, "Sociology" (code 2200); seventh, "Political Science" (code 2800); and eighth, "Arts" (code 2900).

There are no real surprises in this particular ranking of undergraduate majors, except perhaps that philosophy shows a strength far beyond the popularity of philosophy departments on most undergraduate campuses. Clearly, systematic theologians tend to be drawn into the discipline by way of an early interest in philosophical thought. This may be significant in several ways. From one perspective it may mean that contemporary systematic theologians have an educational background which is generally in line with the traditions of the past. Philosophy has clearly been the most common "pre-theological" or preparatory discipline for theologians as long as formal processes of education have existed. From another perspective it may mean that systematic theology is once more a discipline that is capable of attracting the liberated mind. Modern philosophy departments do not consider

54

Table 18

Undergraduate Majors, Systematic Theologians*
(Number of systematic theologians for each category)

Ranking	Code levels	Single Concentration	In Combination		Total	Percentage
			Primary	Secondary		
I. General Areas and Groups of Disciplines:						
1. Sciences in General	(2000)	386	95	63	544	87.60%
2. Sciences of Religion	(3000)	18	3	23	44	7.09%
3. Biblical Studies	(4000)	9	1	7	17	2.74%
4. Theological Studies	(5000)	4		5	9	1.45%
5. Historical Studies	(6000)	6			6	0.97%
6. Practical Studies	(7000)			1	1	0.16%
					621	
II. Specific Subjects, Subject Areas, or Disciplines+						
1. Sciences in General: Philosophy	(2600)	172	21	43	236	38.00%
2. Sciences in General: Languages, Literature	(2400)	94	48	3	145	23.35%
3. Sciences in General: History	(2500)	38	14	9	61	9.82%
4. Sciences in General: Natural & Physical Sciences	(2700)	25	1	4	30	4.83%
5. Sciences in General: Psychology	(2300)	9	7		16	2.58%
6. Sciences in General: Sociology	(2200)	10	4		14	2.25%
7. Sciences in General: Political Science	(2800)	10		2	12	1.93%
8. Sciences in General: Arts	(2900)	8		2	10	1.61%

*Total number included: 522
+Total number of subject codes: 143
 Total referred to in this context: 23

themselves "pre-theological" in the traditional sense; philosophy majors are not now surrounded by an intellectual atmosphere generally friendly to theology. If they come through to involvement in systematic theology against a background in modern philosophical studies, they would therefore tend to be the type of theologians who are eager to do theology in open and honest encounter with the philosophical perspectives of our time. As we shall see in other contexts below, this is indeed the orientation of North-American systematic theologians at the present.

Theological Seminaries

We shall proceed now to two inquiries regarding the second step in the training of systematic theologians--the graduate-professional level, or what is normally described as the theological school or seminary. We are interested first in identifying the schools that have played a major role in the development of those who are now active in the discipline, and we shall secondly present an overview of the subjects or subject areas which seem to have formed the most common focal points or areas of concentration for students who eventually moved into active participation in the discipline of systematic theology.

Of the 560 persons we have surveyed in this study, 67 individuals or 11.96% of North-American systematic theologians list no seminary at all. Of the rest, 318 persons or 56.70% have attended one such institution; 53 persons or 9.46% have attended two; and 10 persons or 1.79% have attended three. Altogether 230 different schools are represented in this material. The majority of these have been attended by a single person represented in our sample, and a number of other schools have 2 or 3 graduates represented in the discipline of systematic theology at the present time. The list of schools that have contributed 4 or more graduates to the North-American community of systematic theologians includes 31 schools. These are listed, ranked by the number of graduates contributed, in Table 19 (page 55a). The table indicates also what type of schools they are--independent, denominational Protestant, or Roman Catholic.

Ranking first on this list, with 35 graduates in the discipline, is Yale Divinity School. No other school even approximates the number of students that have gone on to professional involvement in systematic theology from this one institution. What this says about the orientation of that school and the impact of those who teach in this field on that faculty is of course only a matter of conjecture in this context, but it seems safe to say

Table 19

Theological Seminaries, Systematic Theologians

Ranking	Number of Graduates		Independent	Denominational (Protestant)	Roman Catholic
1.	35	Yale University Divinity School	x		
2.	14	Pontifical Gregorian University (Rome)			x
3.	13	Union Theological Seminary (NY)	x		
4.	12	Woodstock College (MD)			x
5.	11	Princeton Theological Seminary		x	
		Southern Baptist Theological Seminary (KY)		x	
7.	8	Boston University School of Theology		x	
		West Baden College (IN)			x
9.	7	Catholic University of America (IL)			x
		Garrett Theological Seminary (IL)		x	
		Harvard Divinity School	x		
		Luther Theological Seminary (MN)		x	
13.	6	Concordia Seminary (MO)		x	
		Candler School of Theology, Emory Univ.		x	
		General Theological Seminary (NY)		x	
		Perkins School of Theology, SMU (TX)		x	
		University of Chicago Divinity School (IL)	x		
		Weston College School of Theology (MA)			x
19.	5	Chicago Theological Seminary (IL)			x
		Dallas Theological Seminary (TX)	x		
		Drew University Theological School (NJ)		x	
		Duke University Divinity School (NC)		x	
		Lutheran School of Theology at Chicago (IL)		x	
		St. Mary of the Lake Seminary (IL)			x
		Southwestern Baptist Theological Seminary (TX)		x	
		United Theological Seminary (OH)		x	
27.	4	Emmanuel College of Victoria Univ. (CAN)			x
		Fuller Theological Seminary (CA)	x		
		Lutheran Theological Seminary (PA)		x	
		St. Mary College (KS)			x
		Union Theological Seminary in Virginia		x	

that the recruitment of candidates for graduate study and teaching in systematic theology from the Yale Divinity School has been impressively strong so far as the current generation of systematic theologians is concerned. In terms of numbers, of the 493 seminary-trained systematic theologians active in North America at this point in time, 7.1% went through seminary at Yale.

A number of other seminaries or theological schools have also contributed significant numbers of graduates to the discipline--five schools are in fact listed with from 11 to 14 former students among the scholars presently active in systematic theology. These are the Pontifical Gregorian University in Rome, with 14; Union Theological Seminary in New York City, with 13; Woodstock College in Maryland, with 12, and Princeton Theological Seminary and Southern Baptist Theological Seminary, both with 11 graduates in the discipline.

It is interesting to observe that although the four top-ranking schools in this context include two independent seminaries (Yale and Union) and two Roman Catholic institutions (Gregorian University and Woodstock College), the list includes an impressively large number of Protestant denominational seminaries as well. In fact, of the 31 schools listed in Table 19, 16 are Protestant denominational schools; 9 are Roman Catholic; and 6 are independent institutions. Obviously, many systematic theologians are recruited for professional involvement in the discipline from within the various theological traditions and in schools that are more explicitly related to the ongoing ministry of the denominations. One cannot say, of course, how explicitly the theological traditions of a denomination inform the systematic theology being taught in denominational seminaries; many of these schools employ teachers of theology that are more ecumenically oriented. But that scholars recruited for the discipline in these contexts are more aware of the particular emphases and orientations of their respective denominational traditions seems natural. The seminary level seems in fact to be the point in their development where systematic theologians do get to give the doctrinal traditions of their denominations some concentrated attention. On the graduate level, as we shall see below, the ecumenical perspectives seem to come more to the forefront.

Areas of Concentration, Seminary

When we come to analyze the areas of concentration chosen by those who are now active as professional systematic theologians while they were yet students in seminaries or theological schools, we begin to get a clearer picture of the process of professional formation through which they have passed. We should note that many systematic theologians--67 of the 560 included in our study--have not attended seminary at all, and that a similar number of people--69 to be exact--who have attended seminary have not reported any particular area of concentration. Our material at this point thus includes only 424 people to whom the inquiry is revelant. This is still sufficient to indicate certain significant tendencies and trends, however, and the fact that 69 seminary graduates report no specific area of concentration may itself be a significant indicator of sorts.

Table 20 (page 57a) is an overview of the responses we have received regarding seminary areas of concentration. It shows first the relative strength of the eight general areas or groups of disciplines, and secondly the most common specific subjects, subject areas, or disciplines chosen for seminary concentration by systematic theologians. Both parts of the overview rank the various code levels and subject codes according to the total number of systematic theologians who report areas of concentration in each, either singularly or in combination with other subjects or subject areas.

Clearly, the single most predominant seminary-level area of concentration for systematic theologians is "Theological Studies" (code level 5000). "Historical Studies" (code level 6000) and "Biblical Studies" (code level 4000) run a distant second and third among the eight major general areas and groups of disciplines. This is entirely in line with the expectations; seminary programs of study--particularly those in America--do tend to be structured so as to facilitate both a certain level of eclecticism and an orientation to professional interests, and one would assume that those who are heading for a career as systematic theologians would want to lay the groundwork for this by concentrating on theology even during their seminary years.

The amount of concentration allowed in a seminary area of concentration varies, of course, widely. Many theological schools have gone to a fairly open curriculum, allowing students a great deal of flexibility as to the areas to be covered and the extent of attention to be given each. Theology concentrations in these contexts could well be quite intensive. Other schools have a curriculum that presupposes a greater distribution of courses and thus provides less opportunity for extensive study in a single field; a theology concentration in such contexts might simply mean that the small number of free elective courses allowed within the curriculum would be taken in the general area of theology.

Table 20

Areas of Concentration, Seminary, Systematic Theologians*
(Number of systematic theologians for each category)

Ranking	Code Levels	Single Concentration	In Combination Primary	In Combination Secondary	Total	% of all References
I. General Areas and Groups of Disciplines:						
1. Theological Studies	(5000)	255	25	50	330	64.08%
2. Historical Studies	(6000)	29	2	28	59	11.46%
3. Biblical Studies	(4000)	21	27	2	50	9.71%
4. Sciences of Religion	(3000)	15	9	3	27	5.24%
5. Sciences in General	(2000)	9	16	1	26	5.05%
6. Practical Studies	(7000)	9	1	5	15	2.91%
7. Systematic/Dogmatic Sub.	(8000)	2	1	2	5	0.97%
8. Prolegomena	(1000)		3		3	0.58%
					515	
II. Specific Subjects, Subject Areas, or Disciplines:**						
1. Systematic Theology	(5400)	123	12	15	150	29.13%
2. Philosophy	(2600)	9	14	1	24	4.66%
3. Moral Theology	(5600)	10	1	7	18	3.50%
4. Biblical Theology: New Testament	(4520)	6	9	1	16	3.11%
5. Philosophy of Religion	(3400)	7	6	2	15	2.91%
6. History of Doctrine	(6300)	6		7	13	2.52%
Church History	(6200)	5	1	7	13	2.52%
8. Philosophical Theology	(3500)	8	2		10	1.94%

*Total number included: 424
**Total number of subject codes: 143
 Total referred to in this context: 41

One might perhaps want to reflect on the wisdom of allowing such concentrations at all on the graduate-professional level, especially in regard to students who are planning to go on to graduate work in preparation for a teaching career in systematic theology. Does a theology concentration in seminary tend to short-change the sytematicians in areas that are manifestly correlative to the role of an integrative scholar? What happens to a systematic theologian who has not had opportunity--or who has not been required--to give equal attention to historical studies, biblical studies, the sciences of religion, and practical studies, during the preparatory phases of his formation as a scholar? Will he tend to consider the discipline of systematic theology as an autonomous and isolated field of study, without deep roots in--or extensive cross reference to-- these other fields of scholarship?

As we shall see below, on the graduate level of the preparation process systematic theologians definitely show a broader spectrum of academic involvements. The impression of a narrowing in the concept of the discipline which may have been received in the context of this present inquiry will thus need to be adjusted when we proceed to analyze the areas of concentration chosen by systematic theologians during their graduate programs. On the face of it, however, it seems somewhat incongruous for the theology concentration to dominate so strongly on the seminary level-- on the broader, more introductory level of theological education--and for the other concentrations, primarily historical studies and the sciences of religion, to come more strongly to the forefront on the graduate level-- where the systematician would be expected to have reached the highest possible pitch of concentration in his primary theological discipline. This incongruity may well be a symptom of a fundamental weakness in the formation process on North-American systematic theologians. It bears on the lack of close integration between seminary-level studies and graduate-level work, and it has to do with the almost total absence in American theological education of the kinds of studies which were traditionally referred to by that ominous-sounding phrase "theological propaedeutic." We shall return to these matters below, in the context of the analysis of the evaluation of the present state of the discipline; we shall find a number of systematic theologians to be seriously concerned with the definition of the discipline, with the clarification of its relationship to other theological and "pre-theological" disciplines, and with the fundamental pedagogical questions related to the structuring of a sound, logical, and progressive process of theological formation for systematicians.

Table 20, Part II, adds some interesting details to the analysis of seminary-level areas of concentration among systematic theologians in North-America. It shows the particular subjects or subject codes which

rank highest on an individual basis. The first ranking, expectedly, goes
to "Systematic Theology" (code 5400). But in second place--though only
a weak second--comes "Philosophy" (code 2600); third ranking goes to
"Moral Theology" (code 5600); fourth, to "Biblical Theology: New Test-
ament" (code 4520); fifth to "Philosophy of Religion" (code 3400); sixth,
a tie between "History of Doctrine" (code 6300) and "Church History"
(code 6200); and eighth, to "Philosophical Theology" (code 3500). The
list thus strengthens the impression of the domination of theology--speci-
fically systematic theology--even on the seminary level, but it indicates
also that a number of people have laid the foundation for their involvement
in the discipline by concentrating their seminary-level studies in philosophical, biblical, and historical subject areas. The balance between the
attention given to these other areas and the attention given to systematic
theology during the seminary years cannot, of course, be determined on the
basis of this material; a detailed study of the core curriculum and the regu-
lations concerning seminary-level areas of concentrations would be required
to be able to speak authoritatively of the situation. But that most systematic theologians tend to move in the direction of an early specialization in
their discipline, and that only a few of them spend their seminary years
building competence in the foundational or "pre-theological" disciplines
of study seems clear.

Graduate   Schools

        We come now to the essence and core--the final step and the crown-
ing point--of the systematic theologian's education; it is the last phase in
the process of preparation, the graduate program, leading to that ultimate
distinction which is often referred to by a curiously ghoulish phrase, "the
terminal degree." Several items in our questionnaire were related to this
particular phase in the making of a systematic theologian. We shall need
to analyze the responses in some detail, point by point, in the next several
sub-sections of this chapter. We shall look first at the list of graduate
schools which the North-American systematic theologians of today have
attended; then analyze their areas of concentration; thirdly summarize the
types of academic degrees they pursued; fourthly observe the kind of dissertation topics which they worked on; and finally look at the names of their
dissertation advisors, the teachers that have had more to do with the deter-
mination of scholarly interests and the definition of professional preoccupations among contemporary systematic theologians than anybody else in our
time.

Of the 560 persons surveyed in our study, 12 individuals, or 2.14% have not attended a graduate school at all. Of the rest, 399 persons or 71.25% have attended a single graduate school; 122 persons or 21.79% have attended two different schools; 24 or 4.29% have attended 3; and 3 persons 0.54% have attended 4.

In all, there are 184 different graduate schools referred to in the biographies in the DIRECTORY. Of these, 31 schools or 16.85% of those listed have been attended by a single systematic theologian in our group. Another 101 schools or 54.89% have had two of these people participate in their program at some time or other. The roster over those schools which have guided 3 or more of their students to professional involvement in the discipline of systematic theology includes 52 schools or 28.26% of all the graduate programs listed. Table 21 (page 60a) is a presentation of this roster. It ranks the schools according to the number of active systematic theologians they have produced, and indicates what type of schools they are, whether independent, Roman Catholic, Protestant denominational schools, or state institutions.

In presenting our material in this manner we are not, of course, making any value judgment on the quality of the graduate programs referred to here. The ranking is strictly a quantitative one, based solely on the number of their graduates who have an involvement in the discipline of systematic theology. One may assume perhaps, that there exists a correlation of some kind between the quality of graduate programs and the number of systematic theologians that have been produced by them, but such assumptions must be carefully qualified, and any such correlations must be checked against a number of other factors before they can be validated. We are not in the position here to undertake any such qualitative tests of the relative strength of graduate schools; Table 21 simple summarizes the information we have received in terms of which graduate schools have had what number of systematic theologians in North America as students.

Heading this list, expectedly, is a group of five major graduate programs which includes the Union/Columbia complex in New York City, the University of Chicago/Chicago Divinity School complex, Pontifical Gregorian University (Rome), Yale University, and Catholic University of America (Washington, D.C.). These five programs account for 222 of the 542 systematic theologians on our list who have what we call "terminal degrees"--or an impressive 40.96% of the contemporary scholars of systematic theology in North America. The Union/Columbia program alone has contributed 64 persons or 11.81%, and must therefore be counted as the single most important training ground for systematic theologians during the last 15 or 20 years. The triumvirate of Union, Chicago and Yale together

Table 21

Graduate Schools, Number of Graduates in Systematic Theology

Ranking	Number of Graduates		Independent	Denominational (Protestant)	Roman Catholic	State
1	39 +25 } 64	Union Theological Seminary/Columbia Univ. (NY)	x			
2	26 +21 } 47	University of Chicago	x			
		" " " Divinity School	x			
3	42	Pontifical Gregorian University (Rome)			x	
4	40	Yale University	x			
5	29	Catholic University of America			x	
6	18	Fordham University			x	
		Boston University				x
8	16	Princeton University	x			
9	15	Harvard University	x			
10	13	Duke University	x			
		Marquette University			x	
		Southern Baptist Theological Seminary (KY)		x		
13	12	University of Iowa				x
		Vanderbilt University	x			
15	11	University of Notre Dame			x	
16	10	Claremont Graduate School (CA)	x			
		University of Edinburgh				x
18	9	University of Louvain (Belgium)			x	
		University of Munich (Germany)				x
		Northwestern University	x			
		University of Oxford (UK)				x
22	8	Drew University	x			
		Emory University		x		
		Graduate Theological Union (Berkeley CA)	x			
		Institut Catholique de Paris			x	
26	7	Angelicum University (Rome)			x	
		Pontifical University of St. Thomas Aquinas (Rome)			x	
		University of Tübingen (Germany)				x
29	6	University of Basel (Switzerland)				x
		Hartford Seminary Foundation	x			
		St. Michael's College in Univ. of Toronto (Can)				x
		State University of Münster (Germany)				x
33	5	University of Fribourg (Switzerland)				x
		Loyola University (Chicago)			x	
		University of Ottawa (Canada)				x
		St. Louis University			x	
		Southwestern Baptist Theological Seminary (TX)		x		
38	4	Boston College			x	
		Free University (Amsterdam)		x		
		Pontifical University of the Lateran (Rome)			x	
		Pacific School of Religion (Berkeley)	x			
42	3	Aquinas Institute (IA)			x	
		Cambridge University (UK)				x
		Dallas Theological Seminary		x		
		Lutheran Theological Southern Seminary (SC)		x		
		McGill University (Canada)				x
		St. Mary of the Lake Seminary (IL)			x	
		Union Theological Seminary in Virginia		x		
		University of California (Berkeley)				x
		University of San Francisco			x	
		University of Strasbourg (France)				x
		University of Zürich (Switzerland)				x

account for 151 scholars in the discipline, which if one assumes that graduates of these schools are predominantly Protestant represents an impressive 46.89% of all Protestant systematic theologians in North America. The two major Roman Catholic programs, those of the Gregorian University in Rome and the Catholic University in Washington, D.C., account for 71 scholars or some 30.74% of all Roman Catholic scholars in the discipline active on the North-American continent.

A second-ranking group of graduate schools that have made significant contributions to the development of North American systematic theologians, each producing from 13 to 18 scholars for the discipline, includes Fardham University, Boston University, and Marquette University, three major Roman Catholic schools; Princeton, Harvard, and Duke Universities, major independents with strong historical connections with various Protestant traditions; and Southern Baptist Theological Seminary, the most prominent denominational school of the Southern Baptist Convention. The youngest of all the graduate programs mentioned so far is the one at Duke University. The fact that within 30 years of its inauguration this program has brought forth a relatively high number of systematic theologians signifies that the discipline is now receiving considerable attention outside of its traditional strongholds. Such developments augur well for the future.

An interesting aspect of our overview of graduate schools with more than 3 graduates now active in systematic theology in North America, presented in Table 21, is the fact that a considerable number of North-American scholars in the discipline have attended, and in many instances received their doctoral degrees from, various European universities. Represented on the list, in addition to several Pontifical Universities in Rome, are the Universities of Edinburg, Louvain, Munich, Oxford, Paris, Tübingen, Basel, Münster, Fribourg, Amsterdam, Cambridge, Strasbourg and Zurich. Other universities in Europe and elsewhere are among those that have contributed one or two scholars to the discipline in North America. This clearly represents a significant broadening of the intellectual basis of the discipline of systematic theology as a whole, and it is particularly important for the North American branch of it. If systematic theologians in North America in the past have existed and worked in some degree of isolation from the major centers outside, or have even suffered from a certain inferiority complex in relation to the major scholars and movements of thought in Europe, this cycle of intellectual provinciality and uncertainty seems now to be broken. North American scholars are still largely the junior partners in the total theological enterprise, but the traffic across the Atlantic is no longer limited to European masters coming here for lectures and guest professorships. Interaction between faculties is increasing; North Americans are increasingly being respected in Europe and elsewhere. Once

61

more, these developments augur well for the future.

One final note regarding the nature of graduate programs should
be included here. An analysis of the institutional character of the
schools listed in Table 21 reveals that, on the whole, Roman Catholic
systematic theologians tend to receive their scholarly training in Roman
Catholic centers of learning. Protestants on the other hand tend to disperse over a wider spectrum of educational institutions. A few denominational schools--seminaries and universities--offer graduate programs
of high quality and are attended by developing scholars that have their
background in the respective denomination or have an interest in certain
teachers and/or perspectives currently represented in these schools. But
by far the larger percentage of Protestant graduate students attend independent universities and graduate schools, as well as various interdenominational centers. Growing numbers of Protestants also attend graduate
programs in state universities in North America or abroad. Thus, Protestant systematic theologians today increasingly receive their scholarly
training in ecumenical or even secular academic contexts. No longer are
they groomed for their task within the fold of their own traditions. Roman
Catholic systematic theologians, however, are still very largely the pro-
ducts of Roman Catholic schools.

We shall not reflect further on the possible consequences of such
developments here. We shall, however, want to keep these facts in mind
as we come to look at the prevailing mind-set of contemporary systematic
theologians below.

Areas of Concentration

The second item in our inquiry concerning the graduate studies of
North-American systematic theologians has to do with their areas of con-
centration--i.e. the subjects or subject areas which formed the primary
focus in their graduate programs. We are not at this point considering the
subjects of their dissertations--these will be summarized separately below--
only the general orientations of their programs of study.

Altogether 531 persons provided answers to this particular section
of our questionnaire. Of these, 416 listed a single subject or subject area,
while 115 listed a combination of two or three--in some instances indicating
one primary area and one or two secondary subjects, others making no such
differentiation at all. Table 22 (page 62a) represents an overview of the

Table 22

Areas of Concentration, Graduate Programs of Systematic Theologians*
(Number of systematic theologians for each category)

Ranking	Code Levels	Single Concentration	In Combination Primary	In Combination Secondary	Total	% of Syst. Theologians	% of Subject References
I. General Areas or Groups of Disciplines:							
1. Theological Studies	(5000)	225	51	52	328	61.77%	50.46%
2. Historical Studies	(6000)	71	10	25	106	19.96%	16.31%
3. Sciences of Religion	(3000)	54	27	13	94	17.70%	14.46%
4. Sciences in General	(2000)	26	20	11	57	10.73%	8.77%
5. Systematic/Dogmatic Sub.	(8000)	14		8	22	4.14%	3.38%
6. Biblical Studies	(4000)	13	4	5	22	4.14%	3.38%
7. Practical Studies	(7000)	12	2	5	19	3.58%	2.92%
8. Prolegomena	(1000)	1	1		2	0.38%	0.31%
Total		416			650		
II. Specific Subjects, Subject Areas, or Disciplines:**							
1. Systematic Theology	(5400)	147	31	18	196	36.91%	30.15%
2. Philosophy of Religion	(3400)	20	22	1	43	8.10%	6.62%
3. History of Doctrine	(6300)	21	2	11	34	6.40%	5.23%
4. Moral Theology	(5600)	15	2	16	33	6.21%	5.08%
5. Philosophy	(2600)	19	10	3	32	6.03%	4.92%
6. Philosophical Theology	(3500)	26		4	30	5.65%	4.62%
7. History of Doctrine, Period Studies	(6330–35)	23	1	5	29	5.46%	4.46%
8. Church History	(6200)	6	3	3	12	2.26%	1.85%

*Total number included 531
**Total number of subject codes: 143
Total referred to in this context: 61

various areas of concentration listed and the number of systematic theologians listing them, and it includes the code numbers of each subject or subject area so as to facilitate cross referencing to the full schematic overview of subject areas presented above (page 15 ff.). Table 22 contains, first, a separate listing of the eight over-all divisions or types of disciplines, ranked in view of the number of people having chosen areas of concentrations within each, singularly or in combination with other disciplines; and it contains, secondly, a list of the specific subjects or subject areas most commonly referred to as areas of concentration, ranked in the same manner.

As Table 22 shows, the clear majority of systematic theologians in North America have come into the discipline by way of graduate programs with an area of concentration in "Theological Studies" (5000-level codes). A total of 328 persons or 61.77% of the entire group had their areas of concentration in this field, either singularly or in combination with other fields. In addition, some 22 persons or 4.14% of the total number had concentrations in the area of "Systematic/Dogmatic Subjects" (8000-level codes)--subjects which of course also fall within the general perimeters of theological studies as well.

The next two most common fields from which areas of concentration are chosen are "Historical Studies" (6000-level codes) and "Sciences of Religion" (3000-level codes). These are listed by 106 persons or 19.96%, and 94 persons or 17.70%, respectively. Also a comparatively large number of systematic theologians have chosen concentrations among "Sciences in General" (2000-level codes), primarily in philosophy; 57 persons or 10.73% of the group as a whole list such concentrations. In comparison, only a relatively small number of systematic theologians have listed areas of concentration in "Biblical Studies" (4000-level codes) and in "Practical Studies" (7000-level codes); only some 20 persons or 3.77% of the total group here had concentrations in each of these areas.

This overview may not at first glance contain any surprises to the initiated. It seems to say, what is already generally recognized in the discipline, that although a majority of systematic theologians still prepare themselves for a scholarly career in the discipline by concentrating primarily--perhaps even exclusively--on theological studies, many of them also lay the groundwork for an involvement in systematic theology by way of historical studies (primarily history of doctrine), the sciences of religion (primarily philosophy of religion and philosophical theology), and the sciences in general (primarily philosophy). This is clearly in line with the way the discipline has been understood, and how systematic theology for this reason has been approached, ever since the beginning of the modern era. At least since Schleiermacher, systematic theologians have generally recognized that their discipline is closely related to a number of other, correlative, "pre-theological" disciplines of study and that it must be pursued, therefore, not in isolation from these other areas of knowledge, but in close correlation with them. The fact that a relatively large number of contemporary systematic theologians have come into the discipline against the background of graduate school concentration in these correlative areas or disciplines may in fact be taken to mean that the validity of the modern perspective is now widely acknowledged and that systematic theology is considered, not as an autonomous, independent and exclusive endeavor that can be undertaken solely on the basis of perspectives and presuppositions laid down within theology itself, but on the contrary, as an inclusive, integrating kind of endeavor--one that must utilize the perspectives and relate to the insights of all other disciplines which in one way or another deal with the history and phenomenology of religious life. At least some of the people involved seem to see it this way.

When this is said, however, it is nevertheless necessary to point out that while some contemporary systematic theologians have come to acknowledge that the discipline has its roots, not only in theology, but over a wide spectrum of correlative subject areas and disciplines of study, the correlations with such areas of concentrations as biblical studies and practical studies-- of the various dimensions of Christian ministry--are obviously not at the present as broadly recognized as the correlation with various historical, scientific, and philosophical areas of study seem to be. Apparently, systematic theologians still have considerable difficulty in establishing a positive relationship with biblical scholarship and pastoral theology. Thus, the broadening of the basis of the discipline which is represented by graduate study concentrations outside of theological studies per se has gone for the most part in the direction of history of doctrine, the scientific study of religion, and philosophy of religion, not toward reintegration with biblical studies and practical concerns of Christian ministry.

The second part of Table 22 presents an overview of the specific subjects or subject areas--disciplines--which have been most frequently listed by those whose graduate school concentrations apparently were most clearly defined or most sharply circumscribed. It gives us a picture of the particular disciplines within each general area of study that have received the most intense attention during the graduate programs of present-day systematic theologians in North America. Not unexpectedly, "Systematic Theology" (code 5400) comes off the winner by a wide margin. Ranking number 2 on the list is "Philosophy of Religion" (code 3400); number 3, "History of Doctrine" (code 6300); number 4, "Moral Theology" (code 5600); number 5, "Philosophy" (code 2600); number 6, "Philosophical

64

Theology" (code 3500); and number 7 and 8, "History of Doctrine: Period Studies" (code 6330) and "Church History" (code 6200).

Once more we observe the strong predominance of theology concentrations, and now in the specific form of systematic theology--in fact, of the 328 persons who during graduate school chose concentrations in the general area of theological studies, 196 or 59.76% indicate that they focused on systematic theology. Another 33 persons or 10.06% have listed specific concentrations in moral theology. The rest of the overview shows the predominance of history of doctrine and church history among the disciplines of historical study chosen and the primacy of philosophy of religion and philosophical theology among the disciplines in the general sciences of religion.

We should observe that this list of specific subjects or subject areas only includes those that are most frequently chosen as concentrations by the systematic theologians whose graduate programs seem to have been most sharply delimited. It represents, therefore, a rather incomplete picture. We shall not on this basis alone be able to make any judgments regarding the nature of graduate programs or their effect on individual systematic theologians or on the discipline of systematic theology as such. However, in comparing the list in Table 22, Part II, with the general overview of subject areas and disciplines included in the Introduction (pp. 15 ff.), one may be inclined to think that the present generation of systematic theologians in North America have come through graduate programs that cluster around a relatively limited number of subjects, and that a large number of subject areas and disciplines have been left to one side altogether. This impression remains, even where all the subject areas of graduate school concentrations are counted; we find, in fact, that only 61 out of the total of 143 categories included in the general overview are referred to. Nevertheless, our impressions must be checked against several other considerations--and most immediately the overview of dissertation topics, to be presented in Table 24, below (p. 68a). Any final judgment on the question whether North-American systematic theologians on the whole show a bias for or against certain subjects or subject areas must be reserved until we have before us the complete collation of all the contexts in which inquiries have been made relative to the subjects or subject areas involved. This collation is presented in Table 39 (pp. 111a-d), below.

Before we get down to that, however, several additional analyses must be presented--and first, a short overview of the kinds of terminal degrees (that phrase again) which have been pursued or the academic credentials which are now held by North-American systematic theologians.

65

Terminal degrees vary, of course, widely, both in nonmenclature and in content. An appendix in the DIRECTORY OF SYSTEMATIC THEOLOGIANS IN NORTH AMERICA contains the acronyms of 49 different degrees (graduate and undergraduate) held by those listed in that volume. At this point we are interested only in surveying the highest academic degree held by each individual systematician, yet even here we find them to be of numerous and varied kinds--22 different terminal degrees are listed, to be exact.

Table 23, (page 66a) is a graphic presentation of the various higher academic degrees--several kinds of doctorates as well as certain other classes of degrees, such as MAs, ThMs and equivalents, and MDivs and equivalents--and the number of systematic theologians who hold them. The overview shows that of the 556 persons who provided information on this point, 11 individuals hold two or more such degrees, causing the total of terminal degrees held by the group as a whole to reach 568. Of these, 529 or 93.13% of all degrees held or presently pursued by systematic theologians are doctorates of one kind or another; 23 degrees or 4.05% of the total are masters degrees; and 16 or 2.82% represent various forms of basic professional degrees for clergy (MDivs, STLs and equivalents).

A comparison of the number of persons holding the various kinds of terminal degrees shows that the most common one, by far, is the PhD degree; 282 persons presently hold this degree, and 26 more are presently pursuing work toward it, all of which adds up to 308 persons or an impressive 55.40% of all North-American systematic theologians listing this particular degree. The PhD degree is of course primarily a university degree, and an Anglo-Saxon one at that. It is normally offered under the auspices of a university graduate school and involves studies not only in several theological disciplines but in a "minor" discipline related to other university departments as well.

Two other doctoral degrees are quite common among systematic theologians also, namely the STD degree (Doctor of Sacred Theology) which is given primarily in Roman Catholic institutions of higher education, and the ThD degree (Doctor of Theology), which is offered for the most part in certain denominational or interdenominational schools that are not related to a university graduate school. 85 persons included in our study hold the STD degree, and another 10 are presently working toward it, making a total of 95 persons or 17.09% of all North American systematic theologians

Table 23

Terminal Academic Degrees, Systematic Theologians

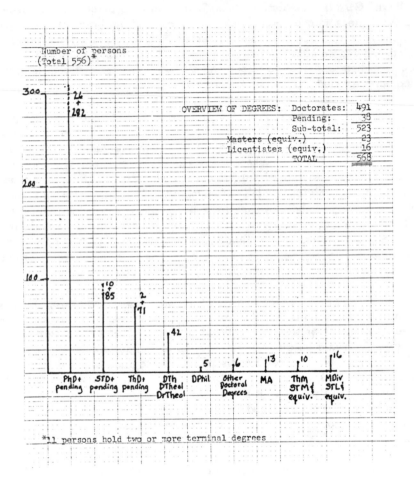

Number of persons
(Total 556)*

OVERVIEW OF DEGREES: Doctorates: 491
                                Pending: 38
                               Sub-total: 523
                        Masters (equiv.)   23
                        Licentiates (equiv.) 16
                                  TOTAL   568

*11 persons hold two or more terminal degrees

who have chosen this particular terminal degree. The corresponding numbers for the ThD degree are 71, plus 2 pending, equalling 73 persons or 13.13% of the total group listing this degree.

Another group of systematic theologians list doctorates designated as DTh, DTheol, or DrTheol, degrees that for the most part are offered in continental European faculties of theology. 42 persons or 7.55% of North American systematicians hold these types of degrees. Additionally, a few people list DPhil degrees and other types of doctorates. No degree given honores causa are included in our survey. Only a small group of systematic theologians list masters degrees or basic professional degrees for clergy as their highest degrees; altogether 39 persons or 7.01% of the total group hold such pre-doctoral terminal degrees.

All in all, the academic credentials of professional systematic theologians in North America appear impressive. Particularly interesting is the high number of PhDs in the group. As we indicated above, in the context of the analysis of areas of concentration, most of these theologians have gone through graduate programs with a focus on theological studies, yet many also have had concentrations in other correlative fields such as historical studies (primarily history of doctrine) and the sciences of religion (primarily philosophy). We considered this a sign of the general recognition that systematic theology is not an exclusive, isolated discipline, but is rather broadly related to a number of other, correlative, even "pre-theo-logical" disciplines of study. When we consider the fact that PhD degrees normally involve studies in a "minor" field--and usually in a department outside the graduate school of religion altogether--this broadening of the academic basis of those involved in systematic theology at the present is shown to be even more prevalent than can be deduced from the listing of graduate school areas of concentration. In my own case, for example, the DIRECTORY lists systematic theology as my area of concentration in gradu-ate school. But my PhD program involved studies in 4 different areas within the graduate school of religion, plus a minor in the department of philosophy. This is not untypical at all.

In the context of the overview of academic degrees, therefore, we find another indication that systematic theologians of today approach their discipline with perspectives oriented to the view that systematic theology must be done, not in splendid isolation from, but in clear correlation with a number of other disciplines of study. If in addition to the general infor-mation which we have regarding graduate school concentrations and degrees we had the necessary information to undertake an analysis of the entire structure of the graduate programs of systematic theologians, we should probably find that as a group the people involved in this discipline have a broader background than most other professional groups in the discipline of religious studies. But even without this information, it seems safe to say that systematic theology is now broadly recognized as an inclusive, integrating kind of discipline.

Dissertation Topics

When we come to analyze the information we have received on the dissertation topics of North-American systematic theologians, another aspect of the picture comes into focus. We are once more faced with what appears to be tendency among systematic theologians—at least as far as their graduate studies are concerned—to be preoccupied with a relatively limited number of subject areas and virtually to ignore large portions of the subject spectrum. The details are as follows:

Of the 560 systematic theologians we have surveyed, 515 have already written academic dissertations of one kind or another—all doctoral dissertations: 491 persons in this group already hold their doctorate, another 38 are presently working on it. When the 515 dissertation topics are categorized and collated, they are found to relate only to 71 of the 143 categories included in our over-all subject scheme—i.e. only half of the total spectrum of subjects, subject areas, and disciplines that are considered relevant to systematic theologians are considered at all in the dissertation topics of systematic theologians.

This aspect of the picture becomes clearer still when we study the distribution and numerical strength of the various subject categories represented by or referred to in the dissertation topics listed. Table 24 (page 68a) presents two separate overviews that are relevant at this point. Part I is a comparison of the eight general subject areas or groups of disciplines, ranking them according to the number of dissertations related to each. Part II looks at the specific subjects, subject areas, or disciplines that have drawn the greatest number of scholars, ranking them according to the number of dissertations related to each. A special feature in both of these overviews is the inclusion of separate columns that provide a breakdown of the total number of dissertations related to each subject category, showing how many dissertations have the subject as their sole focus and how many consider the subject in combination with some other subject category, and in the case of combinations, how many dissertations have the subject as their primary focus and how many relate to it only secondarily.

Table 24

Dissertation Topics, Systematic Theologians*
(Number of dissertations for each category)

Ranking	Code Levels	Single Concentration	In Combination Primary	Secondary	Total	% of all Sub. References
I. General Areas or Groups of Disciplines:						
1. Historical Studies	(6000)	100	307	293	700	82.45%
2. Systematic/Dogmatic Sub.	(8000)	23	12	5	40	4.71%
3. Prolegomena	(1000)	3	2	21	26	3.06%
4. Sciences of Religion	(3000)	18	4	3	25	2.94%
5. Theological Studies	(5000)	13	4	1	18	2.12%
6. Biblical Studies	(4000)	13	2	1	16	1.88%
7. Practical Studies	(7000)	6	1	7	14	1.65%
8. Sciences in General	(2000)	4	2	4	10	1.18%
Total		180			849	
II. Specific Subjects, Subject Areas, or Disciplines**						
1. History of Doctrine: Motif Studies	(6320)	5	2	267	274	32.27%
2. History of Doctrine: Studies of Individual Theologians	(6370)	52	171	11	234	27.56%
3. History of Doctrine: Comparative Studies	(6380)	8	57	6	71	8.36%
4. History of Doctrine: Tradition Studies	(6350)	13	32	4	49	5.77%
5. History of Doctrine Period Studies	(6330)		20	15	35	4.12%
6. Theological Methodology: Approaches	(1220)	2	2	12	16	1.88%
History of Ideas: Modern Period	(6130)	11	4	1	16	1.88%
8. Biblical Theology: Thematic Studies	(4530)	9	1	1	11	1.30%
9. Philosophy of Religion: Religious Language	(3420)	4	3		7	.82%
10. Theological Ideology (Points of View)	(1500)			6	6	.71%
Doctrine of Christ	(8300)	1	4	1	6	.71%
12. Psychology of Religion	(3300)	2	1	2	5	.59%
Philosophical Theology: Theistic Studies	(3510)	5			5	.59%
Philosophical Ethics	(3600)	4		1	5	.59%
Total		116				

*Total number included: 515
**Total number of subject codes: 143
Total referred to in this context: 71

Both tables show the indisputable priority of historical studies in the choice of dissertation topics among North-American systematic theologians--the predominance of such subjects is in fact astounding. Of the eight general areas of study or groups of disciplines listed in Table 24, Part I, "Historical Studies" (code level 6000) is so far out ahead as to outstrip all the others combined by 100 to 80 in the column showing the number of dissertations with a single-code subject, and by much larger margins in the columns showing the number of dissertations with two or three-code combination subjects. Of the 335 dissertations in these columns, 307 have a primary focus in "Historical Studies," 293 a secondary focus. Over-all, subjects or subject areas in "Historical Studies" are referred to, singularly or in primary or secondary combinations with other subjects, 700 times in the 515 dissertation topics surveyed, compared with only 150 references altogether to other parts of the subject spectrum.

The most disappointing aspect of the overview of dissertation topics presented in Table 24, Part I, is the fact that the 8000 code level, "Systematic/Dogmatic Subjects", and the 5000 code level, "Theological Studies", are so little in evidence. Significantly, "Systematic/Dogmatic Subjects" does represent the second-ranking general area; 40 academic dissertations or 7.77% of the total surveyed prove to have a relationship of one sort or another to this particular part of the subject spectrum. But this is a very small number. Only 23 academic dissertations with a single-subject focus--only 4.47% of all the dissertations surveyed--had their focus in any of the 33 individual subject categories in this particular area, and only 17 dissertations with a combination of two or more subjects were related to the specific subject codes included in this area--12 having a primary focus on such subjects, 5 a secondary relation to such subjects. Apparently, very few systematic theologians start their scholarly career in the discipline by writing a dissertation that represents a principal, systematic or constructive explication of a certain part of Christian faith or doctrine. Not even subjects or subject areas within "Theological Studies" generally (code level 5000) seem to draw the attention of dissertation writers in systematic theology to any great extent. The 5000-level subject codes are ranked in 5th place in the overview; only 18 dissertations by North-American systematic theologians are related to subjects, subject areas, or disciplines that belong within "Theological Studies", specifically.

When one looks at Table 24, Part II, the overview of what appears to be the most predominant individual subject codes from across the whole subject spectrum, one finds ranking in positions 1 through 5 several specific subject categories within "History of Doctrine" (code level 6300); tied for 6th place are "Theological Methodology: Approaches" (code 1220) and

"History of Ideas: Modern Period" (code 6130); ranked 8th is "Biblical Theology: Thematic Studies" (code 4530); 9th "Philosophy of Religion: Religious Language" (code 3420); and 10th "Theological Ideology (Points of View)" (code 1500). In 11th place is the first and only subject from either the 8000-level or the 5000-level listed among the 14 leading subject-categories included, namely "Doctrine of Christ" (code 8300). Only a total of 6 dissertations among those surveyed have been related to this subject code; a single dissertation focused on it singularly and 5 dealt with it in combination with other subjects (4 primarily, 1 secondarily). Dominating the list of leading subject categories completely are the five different sub-categories of the history of doctrine which are ranked in position one through five--all of them listed with a total number of dissertations that outstrips the subject codes next in order by margins of from 2:1 to 17:1.

The single subject code with the largest total number of dissertations by systematic theologians related to it is "History of Doctrine: Motif Studies" (code 6320); 274 dissertations or 53.20% of all those surveyed, are related in one way or another to this particular subject category. This may serve to justify to a certain extent the strong predominance of historical studies in the dissertations of North-American systematic theologians; they do, after all, study motifs of thought, many of which are theological--perhaps even specifically doctrinal--motifs. However, only 5 dissertations have had this subject code as their sole focus. Apparently, only a very few systematic theologians have attempted in their dissertations to produce complete historical overviews of various doctrinal motifs as these have been developed throughout the span of time, by various traditions, and in the thought of the theologians who have contributed to it. It is only as a secondary focus in combination with other subject codes that motif studies seem to be plentiful; 267 dissertations, or 51.84% of the total number surveyed, show such motif-studies as being the secondary focus. All in all, then, we find that whatever systematic theologians do in regard to the primary subjects of their dissertations, they do seem to have a secondary interest in identifying and explicating basic theological motifs.

Table 24, Part II, allows us to judge which of the specific subject areas have received the heaviest emphasis both in the dissertations that related to a single subject code and in dissertations that represent a combination of two or more subjects. Among single-subject dissertations, by far the largest number have focused on "History of Doctrine: Studies of Individual Theologians" (code 6370); 52 dissertations, or 10.10% of all the dissertations surveyed, fall within this particular subject code. In addition the same subject category is clearly the largest also in the column covering the primary subject areas of dissertations where two or more subject codes are combined; 171 such dissertations, or 33.20% of all those surveyed, have as their primary focus the study of an individual systematic theologian. In fact among all dissertations that focus on a combination of several subjects or subject areas, the most predominant subject codes are precisely "History of Doctrine: Studies of Individual Theologians" (code 6370)--in the column indicating primary focus--and "History of Doctrine: Motif Studies" (code 6320), in the column showing secondary focus. This, then, accounts for the fact, so clearly evident in the listing of dissertation topics in the DIRECTORY OF SYSTEMATIC THEOLOGIANS IN NORTH AMERICA, that most doctoral candidates in systematic theology seem to formulate dissertation topics that focus on a single theologian and have as their purpose to analyze his particular contributions to the development of certain theological or philosophical motifs.

No further analysis of these aspects of our material shall be attempted here. We would suggest, however, that both future graduate students and dissertation advisors give Table 24 careful scrutiny in comparison with the complete list of subject categories included above (cf. pp. 15 ff.). The result might well be the conviction that academic dissertation topics for systematic theologians in the future need to be conceived along somewhat different lines, and that they must be formulated more consciously in terms of the over-all needs and interests of the discipline.

Dissertation Supervisors

The final aspect of our inquiry concerning the background and training of systematic theologians is an overview of the names of dissertation advisors--the scholars and teachers who have guided and supervised the present community of systematic theologians in North America during the last, crucial stage of their graduate program, the writing of a doctoral dissertation. The list is long, and reads like a who's who of scholars, American and European. In recognition of their impact as teachers we shall include them all here, ranking them by the number of systematic theologians in our survey that have listed them as their dissertation advisors.

Altogether 477 of our respondents have provided us the names of their dissertation advisors. Many of these names are unknown to us, and the information--often handwritten--was almost undecifereable at times. We hope all the names have come out correctly here. There are 350 different names on the list, and duplications are therefore rather unusual--each advisor, in fact, has had only an average of 1.36 of the contemporary systematic theologians in North America writing dissertations under their supervision. There are nevertheless a few of these advisors that stand out among the rest as having had a relatively high number of people now active in the discipline writing their dissertations under them. The list is as follows:

13 advisees:
Gilkey, L.

12 advisees:
Hartt, J.

11 advisees:
Williams, D.D.

7 advisees:
Niebuhr, R.
Pauck, W.

5 advisees:
Berkouwer, G.C.
Brightman, E.S.
Cushman, R.E.
Moody, D.
Pelikan, J.
Tracy, D.
Witte, J.L.

4 advisees:
Frei, H.
Gerrish, B.A.
Lonergan, B.
Meland, B.
Niebuhr, H.R.
Sittler, J.
Tillich, P.
Welch, C.

3 advisees:
Adams, J.L.
Alszeghy, Z.
Bennett, J.
Calhoun, R.
Cobb, J.B.

deLavallette, H.
DeWolf, L.H.
Forell, G.W.
Foster, D.
Godsey, J.D.
Gustafson, J.
Holmer, P.L.
Kerr, H.T.
Lehmann, P.
Loomer, B.
McCue, J.
Neville, R.
Niebuhr, R.R.
Peter, C.
Rahner, K.
Richardson, C.C.
Riggan, G.A.
Runyon, T.H.
Schmaus, M.
Shinn, R.L.
Smith, J. E.
Spalding, J.C.
Torrance, T.F.
Van Roo, W.

2 advisees:
Alfaro, J.
Auer, J.
Austin, C.G.
Baillie, J.
Barnette, H.H.
Barth, K.
Baum, G.
Boyer, C.
Bromiley, G.W.
Brunner, E.
Brunner, P.
Burke, E.

Casserley, J.V.L.

Chadwick, H.

Christian, W.A.

Cousins, E.

Dickie, E.P.

Dietrich, W.

Egan, J.M.

Ehrenstrom, N.

Ferre, N.F.S.

Fries, H.

Gleason, R.W.

Grech, G.

Hendry, G.

Hodgson, P.C.

Hordern, W.

Houssiau, A.

Kaufman, G.

Kilian, S.

Kuenneth, W.

Langford, T.A.

Luthi

McGill, A.

McLelland, J.C.

Michalson, C.

Motherway, T.J.

Nichols, J.H.

Orbe, A.

Outler, A.

Pannenberg, W.

Phillips, G.

Quasten, J.

Rhoades, D.H.

Roberts, D.E.

Scheffczyk, L.

Schilling, S.P.

Spinka, M.

Stevenson, W.T.

Thomas, J.N.

Thompson, B.

Van Oyen, H.

Walgrave, J.

1 advisee:

Achval

Anton, A.

Arnoult, L.A.

Aubert, R.

Baab, O.

Babos, S.

Backman, M.V.

Bainton, R.

Baker, R.A.

Beach, W.

Beardslee, W.A.

Bertocci, P.

Betz, J.

Bilaniuk, P.

Binkley, O.T.

Blanke, F.

Boorman

Boozer, J.

Boyer, L.

Braaten, C.E.

Breen, Q.

Brett, G.S.

Bring, R.

Brown, R.

Browning, D.

Brueggeman, E.

Burns, P.

Canter, N.F.

Carlson, S.

Cappello, F.

Chafer, L.S.

Chavasse, A.

Cone, J.

Connell, F.

Connor, W.T.

Cooke, B.

Damborieha, P.

Danielou, J.

Davies, H.

Degraeve, F.

de Guibert, J.

DeVos, A.

Dewart, L.

Diem, H.

Dillenberger, J.

Doherty, G.
Dombouena, P.
Donahue, J.M.
Dorenzo, J.M.
Dowey, E.A.
Driver, T.
Dunne, J.S.
Egan, K.
Farley, E.
Fennell, W.
Fenton, J.
Feuillet, A.
Findlay, J.N.
Fink, E.
Fiorenza, F.
Flick, M.
Florovsky, G.V.
Friend, H.
Fuerst, C.J.
Ganoczy, A.
Geffre, C.
Gilson, E.
Goergen, D.
Grant, F.C.
Greenslade, S.L.
Grislis, E.
Gurian, W.
Gy, P.
Hamel, E.
Handy, R.
Haroutunian, J.
Harrod, H.
Haring, N.M.
Hauter, C.
Healey, E.
Heaney, J.J.
Hefner, P.
Hendricks, W.L.
Henry, S.
Herberg, W.
Herzog, F.
Herr, J.D.
Hick, J.
Hill, W.

Hiltner, S.
Hitchcock, O.
Hoekendijk, H.
Hoffman, H.
Hoffman, S.
Horvath, A.
Hunt, W.B.
Iserloh, E.
Jacobsmeyer, V.P.
Joest, W.
Jones, J.E.
Jones, J.R.
Jourjon, J.
Kane, W.H.
Kasper, W.
Kavanagh, A.
Kehm, G.
Kelly, B.H.
Kerr, W.
Kiesling, C.
Kinder, E.
Knudson, R.
Kohak, E.
Kristeller, P.O.
Kroner, R.
Küng, H.
Lamirande, E.
Lakner, F.
Latourelle, R.
Lecler, J.
Leith, J.H.
Lesage, G.
Lewis, E.
Lieb, F.
Ligier, L.
Lindbeck, P.
MacKinnon, D.M.
Macquarrie, J.
Marsh, J.
Marthaler, B.
Martin, J.A.
Matson, W.I.
Matthijs, M.
Masson, J.

McCoy, C.	Remick, O.
McNicholl	Richardson, H.
McIntyre, J.	Riddell, J. G.
McNally, R.E.	Ritschl, D.
Meehan, M.	Roberts, D.R.
Menegoz, E.	Robinson, J.M.
Metz, J.B.	Robinson, N.H.G.
Meyer, C.	Ryrie, C.C.
Mihelic, J.	Seasoltz, R.K.
Miller, W.	Scharlemann, R.P.
Mitchell, L.	Schelkle, K.H.
Mooney, C.	Schlink, E.
Muelder, W.	Schoonenberg, P.
Mueller, W.A.	Schupp, F.
Muhlenberg, E.	Sheehy, M.
Muhlenberg, J.	Shepherd, M.H.
Munoz	Siefert, H.
Murray, J.C.	Siegwald
Nelson, J.R.	Skublics, E.
Neunheuser, B.	Songer, H.S.
Noonan, J.T.	Sontag, F.
Norwood, F.	Spicq, C.
Oberman, H.	Spitz, L.
O'Breartuir, L.	Stelling-Michaud, S.
O'Hanlon, D.	Stinnette, C.
Oliver, H.	Sullivan, F.
O'Malley, T.P.	TeSelle, E.
O'Meara, T.	Thielicke, H.
Ommen, T.	Thomas, G.P.
Outka, G.	Thompson, M.
Parvis, M.M.	Trentham, C.
Pelland, L.	Tromp, S.
Phillippee, M.D.	Van Dusen, H.P.
Pittenger, N.	Van Maanen, W.
Plagnieux, J.	Velocci
Polonska-Vasylenko	Vidler, A. R.
Preus, J.	Von Rohr, J.
Price, T.D.	Vorgrimler, H.
Pristl, J.	Walsh, T.
Proudfoot, W.	Walvoord, J.
Puzo, F.	Walz, A.
Range, J.	Watson, P.
Ratschow, C.H.	Weber, O.
Ratzinger, J.	Wells, N.

Whitcomb, J.
Whitehouse, W.A.
Whol, T.
Williams, M.
Wood, H.G.
Wright, J.

Before we make an end to this chapter, let us look back once
more to the question that was raised at its beginning, "How does one
become a systematic theologian?" The answer we have given here is
still not a principal, definitive and absolute one--it is still only of the
order of pointing out how this particular group of systematic theologians
came to be what they are. The answer, therefore, is empirical, descriptive, and analytical, not normative, prescriptive, or synthetic. But this
does not mean that it gives no answer or that it can offer us no guidance.
Much can be learned from observing the lives of others--positive as well
as negative things. We shall hope that those who read these lines will be
able to glean from this chapter some insight into the process by which
systematic theologians are made, and that if they are inclined to follow
in their footsteps they will have a better grasp of the road that lies ahead
of them and the decisions that will be required along the way.

Chapter 3

Systematic Theologians: The Daily Tasks

Part of the myth that has been generally disseminated concerning the daily work of academicians is that they keep short hours and waste much of the time when they do pretend to work. Laymen hear of teaching loads averaging between 8 and 15 hours a week and think this compares favorable even with bankers' hours; they are horrified to learn that professors generally consider a reduction in teaching load a necessary presupposition for making real contributions to scholarship. They do not generally understand the simple fact that for every hour in the classroom, professors normally spend on average of three to four hours in preparation, student consultation, test evaluations, and other class-related activities, and that a 12-hour teaching load thus easily becomes a 48-hour work week. Neither do they usually consider that added to this are the normal professorial responsibilities related to committee assignments, faculty meetings, student advising, and other on-campus activities, by which the work week of academicians becomes more crowded still. And they do not see that with the usual types of off-campus responsibilities added--most colleges and universities having become highly service-oriented in relation to their constituencies or to the community at large in recent decades--the time left over for serious scholarship, research and writing, is understandably rather limited. Academicians know all these pressures; they live with them. Still, the work is all being done, somehow.

It is not our purpose here to offer an apology for the teaching profession--most professors manage to keep most of the balls of their juggler's act together in the air, or in their hands long enough to toss them back into visibility; not often are they found to drop out of their complex routine and cause it all to end in an unmanageable mess. Our purpose in this chapter and the next is to take a closer look at two specific dimensions of the daily work of systematic theologians in North America: their teaching responsibilities and their research interests. This, manifestly, is not all there is to the professional activities of systematic theologians, but the inquiry does relate to the two most important dimensions of their activities as far as the discipline itself is concerned. In fact, our portrait of the current state of the discipline would not be useful without an inquiry into these ongoing activities or without an analysis of the manifestations of systematic theology in actuality and practice which such activities represent.

Our interest in this chapter focuses on several significant details. We shall study first the "range" of teaching in which North-American systematic theologians are presently involved and ask whether the theologians are teaching in predominantly undergraduate, seminary, or graduate school contexts uniquely, or whether they range over a broader spectrum, encompassing several or all three of these contexts. The material brought to light here will give further specificity to the inquiries concerning the present positions of systematic theologians which were included in Chapter 1, above. Our next concern will be the "level" of teaching-- i.e., whether it is predominantly in introductory courses, upper-level courses, select seminars and thesis supervision, or on "other" levels (such as continuing education), or whether it includes several or all of these levels in some recognizeable combination. Thirdly, we shall look at the general "areas" of teaching--i.e., whether systematic theologians tend to orient their teaching singularly toward methodological considerations (principles of theology), historical studies (history of doctrine), systematic studies (constructive theology), or "other" areas (subjects not immediately identified with the former ones), or whether they span a wider spectrum of subject areas, including several or all of those listed here. A fourth section of this chapter will contain an overview of the specific subjects which systematic theologians teach; our purpose here is to gauge what appears to be the main emphases and preoccupations of systematic theologians as teachers at the present. A fifth section gives further details to this overview by looking at the authors and sources which are most heavily used by systematic theologians in their courses. Then, a final section of this chapter focuses on the professional associations of systematic theologians--summarizing the information we have received concerning membership of systematic theologians in major professional societies.

Range of Teaching

Our first concern is to identify the types of teaching situations in which North-American systematic theologians are involved, and particularly to see how widely the teaching involvements of these people range at the present. The categories we are operating with here are three: undergraduate teaching contexts (college and university); seminary contexts (theological schools or professional schools for clergy); and graduate programs (in universities and theological schools). The inquiry is designed to show how many people are involved in a single one of these contexts, and which, and how many systematic theologians range over several of these contexts, and in what sorts of combinations.

The result of such analyses is obviously correlative to our earlier inquiries concerning the present positions of systematic theologians, but the focus here is more specific--namely teaching--and the details, therefore, much clearer. For one thing, we will be able to find out to what extend systematic theologians are liable to be single-track pedogogues, or correspondingly, to what extend they are involved in several different contexts; for another, we will be able to determine whether systematic theology is a discipline that can find a basis in and relation to a broad range of academic contexts, or whether it is primarily at home in a narrower academic setting.

Table 25 (page 80a) is a graphic presentation of the information that bears on these issues. It shows the number of people whose teaching responsibilities fall exclusively in one of the three main contexts--undergraduate, graduate-professional,* and graduate-- and it shows the number of people whose teaching involvements range over two of these--in some combination--or include all three.

As can be seen from this overview, of the 543 systematic theologians who provided the information relevant to this point, 288 or 53.04% teach in a single context; the rest range over a wide spectrum. In the first group, interestingly enough, the largest column is that which shows the number of systematic theologians who teach in an undergraduate setting, exclusively; 143 systematic theologians or 26.34% of all those surveyed belong in this group and thus do their systematic theology within the context of a general liberal arts setting. In some ways, this appears extraordinary. Systematic theology is, after all, a discipline that focuses on the exposition and explication of basic Christian faith and doctrine; it is normally thought of as an activity of scholars who stand within and work on behalf of the church, and is not usually considered the type of discipline that would thrive among the sciences in general and in close correlation with secular reason and intellectual liberalism--or that undergraduates would either have the head or the stomach for.

We shall not, of course, forget that a number of undergraduate schools where systematic theologians are active as teachers are church-related institutions. Nevertheless, the point must be made that significant numbers of systematic theologians now also teach in secular undergraduate contexts. Their impact in those settings is hard to assess, as is the reverse influence of these kinds of contexts on their approach to teaching and their comprehension of the discipline of systematic theology itself. We found in Chapter

---

* This is the term that seems to have gained status recently as the appropriate description of seminaries or theological schools.

Table 25

Range of Teaching, Systematic Theologians

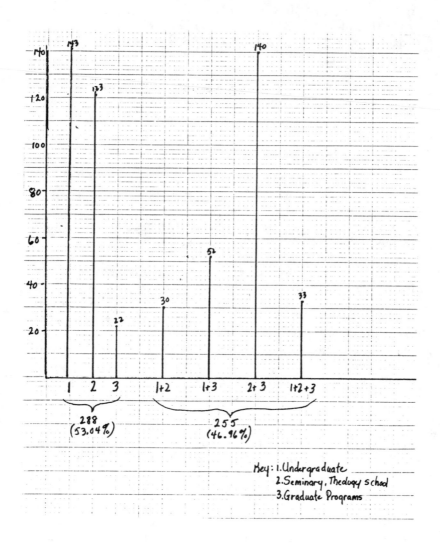

Key: 1. Undergraduate
2. Seminary, Theology school
3. Graduate Programs

2, above, in the analysis of the graduate school concentrations of systematic theologians, that a broadening of the academic groundwork for
an involvement in the discipline has taken place in recent years and that
systematic theology in the modern period has been increasingly recognized as an integrative, inclusive sort of discipline--one that must be
undertaken not only in close correlation with the sciences of religion,
but in interaction with other, "pre-theological" disciplines of knowledge
as well. We find now, additionally, that this broadening is evident in
the range of teaching of systematic theologians, also. And the picture
will be further clarified when we come to consider the specific subjects
which they teach, below.

When we add to the number of systematic theologians who teach in
undergraduate contexts exclusively the number of people whose range of
teaching includes undergraduate contexts, in some combination with graduate -professional and graduate school involvements, the breadth of the
undergraduate teaching of systematic theologians can be appreciated. The
number of people indicating such involvements in undergraduate teaching
to any degree whatever is 255, or a full 46.96% of all the systematic
theologians surveyed.

Several additional features that are concerned with the range of
teaching of North-American systematic theologians come into view in
Table 25. One is the number of systematic theologians who teach in the
graduate-professional context only--123 persons or 22.65% of the group
surveyed are classified as teaching in seminary contexts exclusively. Another is the number of people who indicate that their teaching is done exclusively in the context of graduate programs--22 systematic theologians
or 4.05% of the total sample limit their teaching to this particular setting.
One may assume that these two groups represent the more classical teaching roles of systematic theologians --that of the typical seminary professor
and that of the distinguished mentor of doctoral students. In that case, the
numbers in both of these groups seem surprisingly small. Does this mean,
once more, that systematic theology has to a large extent left the safe and
secure havens, and its privileged position of an earlier day and time, and
that it is now for the most part in the hands of people who are not only required to range more widely in their teaching involvements, but who are
also capable of doing so? This conclusion seems justifiable.

One final point is appropriate in this connection: the integration
of graduate programs and graduate-professional schools of theology is obviously close and strong--140 systematic theologians or 25.78% of our total group indicate that they have dual teaching responsibilities which include both of these contexts. There is a significant group of people, also,

whose teaching includes both the undergraduate and the graduate con-
texts--52 persons or 9.58% of all the systematic theologians surveyed
indicate a range of teaching that spans this spectrum without including
the seminary or graduate-professional context. Another group, namely
33 persons or 6.08% of the people surveyed, teaches over the entire
spectrum--in undergraduate, graduate-professional, and graduate contexts as well. All in all, it appears that graduate programs are not now
the exclusive domain of a select few, highly sophisticated theoretical
scholars who have little "feel" for the realities of life, among undergraduates as well as in the ministries of the church. Such stereotypes are for
all intents and purposes dissolved in the light of the information which we
have presented here.

Levels of Teaching

The purpose of this inquiry regarding the levels of teaching of systematic theologians--besides the obvious one, to give a summary of the
factual information we have received--is to explore to what extent their
teaching responsibilities are limited to a single level, or conversely to find
out to what extend systematic theologians distribute their teaching activities up and down the pedagogical ladder. The categories we have chosen
for sorting out this information are the following four: introductory courses;
upper-level courses; seminars and thesis supervision; and other teaching
activities (primarily continuing education).

A problem which must be acknowledged in developing this material
is that the levels of instruction obviously relate to the different contexts
which we have just looked at. It has not been possible for us to analyze in
detail how the information on teaching levels correlate with the range of
teaching--i.e. how many people who teach exclusively in an undergraduate
setting are primarily involved in introductory courses, or how many systematic theologians who teach in graduate-professional and graduate schools
offer only upper-level courses or seminars. The information we are summa-
rizing here cuts across the entire range of teaching contexts. It is still significant, however, for it does give us an indication of the kind of teaching
which is being done by systematic theologians, in whatever context, and
particularly the extent to which they involve themselves in curricular offerings that provide greater or lesser degrees of accessibility for student popu-
lations and other constituencies.

Table 26 (page 82a) summarizes the information which we received
in response to the inquiry concerning levels of teaching. Separate columns

Table 26

Levels of Teaching, Systematic Theologians

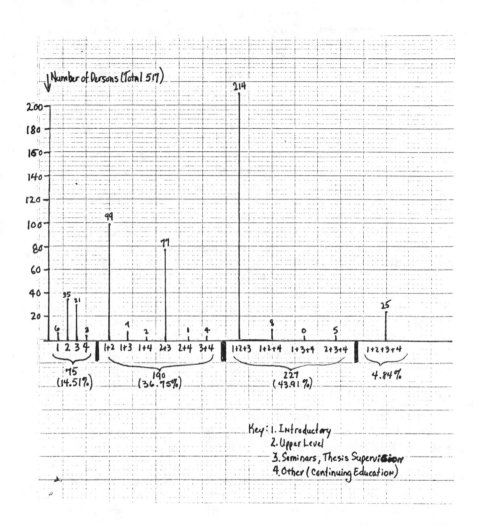

Key: 1. Introductory
2. Upper Level
3. Seminars, Thesis Supervision
4. Other (Continuing Education)

show the number of systematic theologians whose teaching is limited to one of the four levels; other columns represent the number of people who teach on two or three levels, and in what combinations; and a last column shows the number of people whose teaching is distributed over all four levels.

It is immediately apparent from this graphic overview that very few systematic theologians limit their teaching to a single level--only 75 persons or 14.51% or the 517 who responded at this point fall within this bracket. More typical is the distribution of teaching involvements over two levels--190 persons or 36.75% of the total group indicate such dual involvements of one kind or another--or over three--227 persons or 43.91% of the systematic theologians surveyed show one of several possible combinations of three out of the four teaching levels indicated. Only a small group of people--25 persons or 4.84% of our sample--indicated that their teaching includes responsibilities on all four levels.

The most remarkable feature of the graphic overview in Table 26 is the fact that the largest single column, or the largest group of systematic theologians by far, represents the people whose teaching responsibilities include both introductory courses, upper-level courses, and selective seminars and thesis supervision. Altogether 214 persons or 41.39% of the active systematic theologians in North America show themselves to be this versatile and this widely accessible. Another 99 persons or 19.15% indicates that their teaching responsibilities include both intorductory and upper-level courses.

The point should not be missed. It proves that systematic theologians are generally not the one track, highly selective specialists which they are commonly conceived to be; and it means that systematic theology itself is not the kind of discipline that concerns itself only with advanced studies-- intellectual super-structures that come to focus only after the groundwork has been laid, by other disciplines or by subordinate crews that have no other function than to introduce the subject or prepare the mind for it.

Table 26 supports this latter point in another way, also: only 6 persons or 1.2% of the entire group of 517 respondents indicated that they teach exclusively on the introductory level, and only 31 persons or 6.00% teach exclusively on the level of select seminars and thesis supervision. In fact, when one calculates the number of people who teach only in upper-level courses, seminars and thesis supervision, and other endeavors, and who thus have no involvement on the introductory level whatever, one finds that only 157 individuals or 30.37% of the total group are thus removed from introductory-level teaching.

One very general correlation can perhaps be made between the earlier inquiry concerning the range of teaching and the present study of the levels of teaching--though only by projection. As can be seen in Table 25 (page 80a), the clear majority of all systematic theologians have some form of teaching involvement in seminaries or graduate-professional schools of theology, either exclusively or in combination with undergraduate contexts and/or graduate programs. An actual calculation shows that of the 543 persons providing this information, 323 individuals or 59.48% of the total group are presently involved one way or another in seminary teaching. If one calculates on the same basis the number of systematic theologians who have some form of teaching involvement in graduate programs, either exclusively or in combination with one or both of the alternative contexts, one finds that 247 individuals or 45.49% of the systematic theologians polled are presently involved in teaching on the graduate level. When one holds these calculations together with the information regarding levels of teaching that is presented in Table 26, the impression is once more strong that even though most systematic theologians are found to teach in contexts where specialization is most prevalent--in seminaries and graduate schools--this does not on the whole invalidate the impression that they represent a remarkably versatile and broadly accessible group of teachers. On the contrary, projections to that effect spring to light immediately when one considers that the sum of all the columns in Table 26 which shows the number of people who teach only upper-level courses and selective seminars and thesis tutorials comes to only 153 persons or 28.18% of all systematic theologians. A corresponding calculation of the number of systematic theologians who do have some involvement in introductory level teaching shows an impressively large group, 359 persons or 66.11% of the total number of systematic theologians in North America, to be so involved.

Areas of Teaching

We come now to a dimension of this chapter that is more directly related to the content of what systematic theologians teach, not simply the context in or the level at which they do so. Our inquiry is thus proceeding to matters that are more essential to our understanding of the teaching of systematic theology as this is actually done in the classrooms of colleges, seminaries and graduate schools at the present. This section focuses on "areas" of teaching; the next, on the subjects of specific courses; and the next after that, the sources used.

Our reference to "areas" of teaching here refers back to our earlier discussion of the definition of the discipline of systematic theology itself (cf. pp. 8 ff. above). As indicated at that point, we had decided earlier that for our purposes here both the narrower definition of systematic theology--that identifying systematic theology as an autonomous, independent and exclusive discipline focusing on the constructive exposition of basic elements of Christian faith--and the broader definition--that considering systematic theology as in integrating, inter-related and inclusive discipline encompassing several "other" theological, even "pre-theological" considerations--were relevant to our inquiry. The materials we shall look at here will, in fact, tell us the extent to which systematic theologians identify the discipline as either narrow in focus or broad in scope.

The categories and formulations we are operating with here are those we chose at that earlier point as most generally acceptable in describing the various areas that systematic theologians are concerned with: principles of theology (methodology); historical theology (history of doctrine, dogmatics); systematic theology (constructive theology); and other areas (the overview of specific courses in the next section will explain what these are). 541 persons responded to our inquiry concerning teaching areas. No one was asked to prioritize their involvements--the relative weight of each area among North-American systematic theologians on the whole would appear in our summaries clearly enough simply by calculating how many people list themselves as teaching in each area.

Once more we must make clear that we have not attempted to analyze the precise correlations between areas of teaching (subject matter generally) and the earlier overviews of levels and range (contexts) of teaching--we are not determining how many systematic theologians who are teaching in undergraduate contexts on the introductory level focus on this or that subject area, singularly or in combination with other subject areas, etc. The details of such inquiries would probably be interesting, but they would be extremely complex--too complex to be done manually, without the benefit of computer analysis. The material we shall summarize here will not be broken down by reference to such sub-categories; it cuts across the entire spectrum of teaching contexts and includes teaching on all levels. What we are after is simply an impression of what subject areas or combinations of subject areas seem to emerge as most common in the teaching of North-American systematic theologians at the present. This will not only tell us a great deal about what systematic theologians do; it will reveal in further detail how the discipline of systematic theology is itself understood in our time.

Table 27 (page 86a) summarizes this material in a graphic way. Separate columns show how many systematic theologians limit their teaching to one of the four areas; other columns show the number of people whose teaching includes two or three of the areas, and in what combinations, and a last column shows the number of people who are involved in teaching over the entire spectrum.

First to be noted is the fact that relatively few systematic theologians teach in only one of the major subject areas--only 100 out of 541 (18.48%) limit themselves this way, and of these, only 51 persons (or 9.43%) teach solely in category 3, systematic or constructive theology, narrowly defined. Once more we see a symbol of the virtual rejection of the narrow conception of the discipline of systematic theology in our time. This particular situation, in regard to teaching, may of course have several reasons; those who are involved in the discipline may well hold a narrower view of it while yet, of necessity, having to involve themselves in teaching subject areas which they themselves consider outside their primary field. Nevertheless, whether of necessity or by predelection, the vast majority of systematic theologians in North America do teach over a wider spectrum of subjects, and this not only reflects the broader impact of systematic theologians throughout the curriculum of the institutions of higher education in this part of the world; it reflects the broadening understanding of the discipline of systematic theology itself.

The overview in Table 27 reveals this broadening rather dramatically. The columns that show the number of people who teach in a combination of two or three subject areas total 200 persons and 195 persons, respectively, or 36.97% with a two-area combination and 36.04% with a three-area combination. Another 48 persons or 8.87% of all systematic theologians in North America indicate that their teaching spans all four categories, including theological methodology, historical theology, constructive theology, and other aspects of religious studies.

The single, most common combination, clearly, is that which includes the first three areas, methodology, history of doctrine, and systematic theology; 116 persons or 21.44% of the total group are involved in teaching all three. Considerable numbers also teach combinations of historical studies and systematic theology--the numbers here are 70 persons or 12.94%--and methodolical studies and systematic theology--57 persons or 10.54% of the total group are involved in these two areas.

It is interesting, also, to calculate the total number of systematic theologians who are involved in teaching in each of the four major areas, either singularly or in some combination with other areas. Table 28 (page

Table 27

Areas of Teaching, Systematic Theologians
I: Types of Teaching Programs

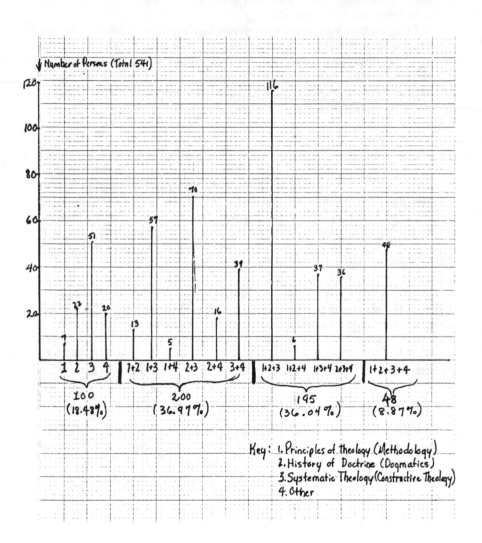

Key: 1. Principles of theology (Methodology)
2. History of Doctrine (Dogmatics)
3. Systematic Theology (Constructive Theology)
4. Other

87a) presents these calculations graphically. For the first area, theological methodology, the total number is 289 persons or 53.42% of the
entire group; for historical theology (history of doctrine, dogmatics),
the total is 327 persons or 60.44%; for systematic or constructive, philo-
sphical theology, the total is 454 persons or 83.92%; and for the other
related subject areas, the total is 207 persons or 38.26%. Clearly, the
teaching of systematic theologians in North America is well distributed
over the entire spectrum of subject areas. Moreover, the balance seems
to be sound. There is a fair amount of attention given to methodological
matters. Not many people focus on principles of theology or theological
methodology exclusively, but more than half of those presently active in
systematic theology in North America involve themselves part of the time
in teaching the presuppositional subject area. Again, while we found in
Table 27 that only 22 systematic theologians limit their teaching to historical theology exclusively, Table 28 shows that over 60% of systematic theologians in North America are involved in teaching subjects related to history of doctrine or dogmatics. The area of systematic or constructive theology is naturally the one receiving the greatest attention in
the teaching of systematic theologians. We saw in Table 27 that 51 persons focus on this area exclusively; Table 28 shows that the vast majority--
83.92% to be exact--of North-American systematic theologians teach
subjects in this area. And other subject areas receive a fair amount of
attention as well; more than a third of the community of systematic theologians in North America teach subjects which go beyond the areas of methodological, historical, and systematic studies. One cannot help being
impressed by the breadth and the balance which characterizes the teaching involvements of this group of scholars. It augurs well both for the
discipline itself, for its integrative role at the present, and for the impact
of systematic theologians on the curricula of educational institutions on
the whole.

Subjects   of   Courses

        This section focuses on the information we have received concern-
ing the specific subjects of courses taught by North-American systematic
theologians at the present. The responses--often full and detailed, but
at times unfortunately rather sketchy--have been analyzed and categorized
according to the overview of subject codes set forth in the introduction
(pp. 15 ff. above). A total of 532 people responded to our inquiries at
this point. The material is thus highly representative of the systematic
theological community as a whole.

Table 28

Areas of Teaching, Systematic Theologians
II: Number of Persons in Each Area

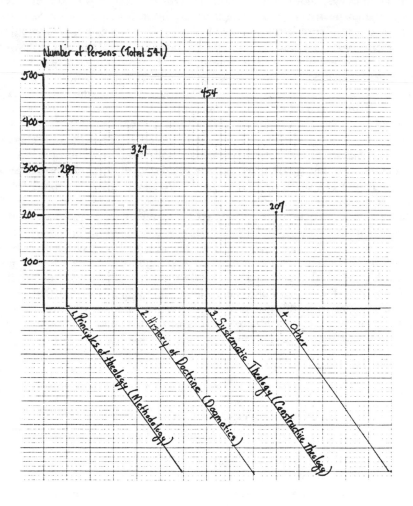

Number of Persons (Total 541)

500 —

454

400 —

329

300 — 289

207

200 —

100 —

1. Principles of Theology (Methodology)
2. History of Doctrine (Dogmatics)
3. Systematic Theology (Constructive Theology)
4. Other

87a

Our summaries here must of necessity be limited to what appears to be general trends and tendencies. We cannot possibly hope to give any detailed picture of the number of subjects or combinations of subject areas which characterize the teaching involvements of various individuals or groups of systematic theologians, or to offer detailed correlations of the information provided at this point with the several variables of range, levels, and teaching areas which we have just looked at, much less with such additional variables as age, years of teaching, areas of concentrations in graduate schools, etc. Such correlations would undoubtedly have been interesting, and had we been able to analyze the materials with the assistance of a computer it would have been a relatively simple matter to produce them.

Even with these limitations, however, we can make some interesting comparisons between the subjects of courses taught by systematic theologians, which are to be set forth here, and the two general overviews of areas of concentration in graduate school programs and subjects of doctoral dissertations which were presented above (cf. Tables 22 and 24, pages 62a and 68a, respectively). But first, let us look at the subjects of courses taught by systematic theologians independently for a moment and attempt to shed some light on the teaching of systematic theology per se.

Table 29 (page 88a) is a summary of this material, first--Part I-- in terms of the eight major areas or groups of subjects, second--Part II-- in terms of the specific subjects, subject areas or disciplines to which courses are related. Both tables rank the various code-levels or the individual subject codes according to the number of systematic theologians offering courses related to them--though Part II lists only the top 20 subject codes.

Table 29, Part I, shows that the courses taught by systematic theologians are well distributed over the entire subject spectrum. Topping the list, expectedly, are the general areas of "Systematic/Dogmatic Subjects" (code level 8000) and "Historical Studies" (code level 6000); 28.94% of all courses listed are related to the first of these, 27.20% to the second. A strong third on the list is the general area of "Theological Studies" (code level 5000); 18.02% of all courses offered by systematic theologians are related to this general category. The subsequent rankings, in order, are fourth, "Sciences of Religion" (code level 3000); fifth, "Prolegomena" (code level 1000); sixth, "Practical Studies" (code level 7000); seventh, "Biblical Studies" (code level 4000); and eighth, "Sciences in General" (code level 2000). Percentages for the leading individual subject codes are included in Table 29, Part II.

Table 29

Subject Areas, Teaching, Systematic Theologians *
(Number of systematic Theologians offering
courses in each category)

I. General Areas:	Codes	Total	% of all Subject Ref.
1. Systematic/Dogmatic Subjects	8000	665	28.94
2. Historical Studies	6000	625	27.20
3. Theological Studies	5000	414	18.02
4. Sciences of Religion	3000	241	10.49
5. Prolegomena	1000	122	5.30
6. Practical Studies	7000	107	4.65
7. Biblical Studies	4000	88	3.83
8. Sciences in General	2000	36	1.57

II. Specific Subjects, Subject Areas or Disciplines:**

	Codes	Total	
1. History of Doctrine, Period: Contemporary	6335	127	5.53
2. Doctrine of Christ	8300	108	4.70
3. History of Doctrine, Studies of Individual Theologians	6370	97	4.22
4. Systematic Theology, Introductory Studies	5410	87	3.79
5. Moral Theology	5600	76	3.31
6. Doctrine of Church	8500	75	3.31
7. Doctrine of Man	8232	71	3.09
8. History of Doctrine, Motif Studies	6320	65	2.83
9. History of Doctrine, School Studies	6360	63	2.74
10. Theological Methodology	1200	62	2.70
11. History of Doctrine, Tradition Studies	6350	61	2.65
12. Philosophy of Religion	3400	60	2.61
13. Systematic Theology	5400	52	2.26
History of Doctrine	6300	52	2.26
15. Doctrine of God	8200	50	2.18
16. History of Religion	3100	49	2.13
17. Theology and Culture	5800	45	2.35
18. Doctrine of Church, Means of Grace	8520	43	1.87
19. Doctrine of Consummation, Eschatology	8700	41	1.78
20. Doctrine of Revelation	8100	38	1.65

* Total number included: 532
* * Total number of subject codes: 143
Total referred to in this context: 116

There are few surprises here, though in the light of what we have seen above it may be significant to point out that Table 29, Part II, shows that systematic theologians are in fact teaching more courses that are related to individual systematic/dogmatic subjects than courses that attempt to cover the entire spectrum of systematic theology or the full sweep of history of doctrine--survey courses which would be related to codes 5400 or 6300. We may be seeing the result of typical North-American approaches to the teaching of systematic theology here. Relatively few systematic theologians have the opportunity, within the curricula and semester schedules of North-American institutions of higher education, to give the kind of massive, sustained attention to a subject which is required in order to cover the full system or the whole history of Christian doctrine. With most courses providing only three or four class hours per week, semesters that are limited to 12 to 18 weeks duration, and with a general disinclination to mounting sequential courses that stretch over two or more semesters, the North-American academic context is understandably more conducive to courses that have a more limited scope. As Table 29, Part II, shows, full survey courses of the type we have referred to here rank relatively low among the individual subject-codes of courses taught by systematic theologians; codes 5400 and 6300 are, in fact, tied for 13th place on the list, with only 52 courses or 2.26% of the total number related to them.

Some further details in Table 29, Part II, are rather interesting. For example, top ranking among the individual subject codes goes to "History of Doctrine, Period Studies: Contemporary Period" (code 6335); the single most popular subject for courses taught by contemporary systematic theologians is thus--what else--contemporary theology! Other sub-categories of the history of doctrine are also ranked high among the top twenty subject codes, namely "Studies of Individual Theologians" (code 6370), ranked 3; "Motif Studies" (code 6320), ranked 8th; "School Studies" (code 6360), ranked 9th; and "Tradition Studies" (code 6350), ranked 11th.

Amont the "Systematic/Dogmatic Subjects" (code level 8000), the highest ranking single subject is "Doctrine of Christ" (code 8300), ranked 2nd over-all; systematic theologians in North America thus prove to be more involved in Christology--at least in so far as teaching is concerned-- than in any other single subject within the Christian system of doctrines. Other sub-categories of systematic/dogmatic subjects are also ranked among the most frequent subjects of courses, namely "Doctrine of the Church" (code 8500), ranked 6th; "Doctrine of Man" (code 8232), ranked 7th; "Doctrine of God" (code 8200), ranked 15th; "Means of Grace" (code 8520), ranked 18th; "Doctrine of Consummation" (code 8700), ranked 19th; and "Doctrine of Revelation" (code 8100), ranked 20th. This shows once

89

more that systematic theologians do indeed teach the classical subjects of Christian theology, although the approach is primarily a piece by piece study of various aspects of the system, not an inclusive, integrating, "systematic" consideration intended to give a full overview of the entire spectrum of Christian doctrine.

As we have already indicated, Table 29, Part I, shows "Theological Studies" (code level 5000) to be the third ranking general subject area in courses taught by North American systematic theologians. When we look at the further information provided in Table 29, Part II, as to the particular subject codes within this area which are most frequently considered in the courses offered, we find that the highest ranking of these particular subject codes is "Systematic Theology, Introductory Studies" (code 5410), ranked 4th over-all; North-American systematic theologians are thus seen to give considerable attention to introductory matters or to questions of methodological importance in the doing of theology. In this connection it should also be noted that code 1200, "Prolegomena, Theological Methodology," ranks high among the specific subjects taught, namely 19th on the list. Other specific subject codes related to "Theological Studies" (code level 5000) rank high among the subjects most frequently referred to in this context also; "Moral Theology" (code 5600) is ranked 5th over-all, and "Theology and Culture" (code 5800) ranks 17th on the list.

If we should undertake, against this background, to compare the results of our analysis of subject areas of courses taught by North-American systematic theologians with our earlier analyses of dissertation topics (Table 24, p. 68a) and areas of concentration in graduate programs (Table 22, p. 62a), several important considerations appear. The comparisons will be clearer when we come to present the complete overview of subjects and subject areas in all contexts, below (Table 39, pp. 111f), but at this point some preliminary observations are relevant.

First, it appears that the teaching involvements of systematic theologians show a better balance between "Systematic/Dogmatic Subjects" (code level 8000) and various types of "Historical Studies" (code level 6000) than appeared in either graduate school concentrations or dissertation topics. In the earlier contexts, code level 8000 ranked a weak fifth and a distant second, respectively, while code level 6000 ranked a strong second and an overwhelming first on the same lists. In the present context the two code levels are just about equal.

We must note, secondly, that although systematic/dogmatic subjects do seem to fare better in the context of the teaching responsibilities of systematic theologians, "systematic theology" narrowly defined (the constructive, integrating and integrated consideration of the entire "system" of Christian doctrine) does not. As we noted earlier, among the areas of concentration in graduate programs, code level 5000--the general area of "Theological Studies", the "parent category" to the specific subject codes listed under the 8000-level codes--is ranked on top. Also, among the individual subject codes ranking highest on the list of graduate school areas of concentration, "Systematic Theology" (code 5400) ranks a strong first. This means that systematic theologians generally do in fact have an educational background that prepares them for teaching a wide spectrum of theological subjects, and that they should therefore be prepared to teach systematic theology "systematically" --in an integrating, constructive fashion. Their dissertation topics, how-ever, were not found to be so oriented; they were primarily and predom-inantly related to historical studies, and most immediately to motif studies (code 6320) and studies of individual theologians (code 6370). Their dissertation research, then, would tend to undergird an approach to teaching that would focus on various facets of the doctrinal spectrum, separately. Our present analysis of teaching subjects shows, as already pointed out, that this is indeed the case. "Systematic Theology" (code 5400) is ranked only 12th among the top 20 subject areas for teaching, while individual doctrines (sub-categories on the 8000 level) are highly visible on the list, and as a group, in fact, rank first. We see, then, that systematic theologians in North America are not, in their teaching, primarily "systematicians." They are more generally teachers of theologi-cal subjects, focusing from time to time on various facets of the doctrinal spectrum and on various dimensions of the history of Christian thought--periods, individual theologians, theological motifs, theological "schools", or traditions of thought. The practical, contextual reasons for this have already been considered; whether there are other, more principal reasons--reasons related to the status of the discipline at the present or to the nature of the discipline itself--is a question we must leave aside for the moment. We shall return to these matters in the context of considering the opinions of systematic theologians concerning the present state of affairs in the dis-cipline, below.

A third observation which is relevant to the comparison of teaching subjects, graduate concentrations, and dissertation topics of systematic theologians has to do with the relative high ranking given the "Sciences of Religion" (code level 3000) in each of these contexts and the relative low priority given to "Biblical Studies" (code level 4000) throughout. We have commented on these features of the contemporary approach to the dis-cipline above (cf. pp. 63 ff.), but they need consideration again--and now by reference to what systematic theologians do and how they have come to be prepared to do it.

As we noted in connection with Table 29, Part I, the "Sciences of Religion" (code level 3000) rank fourth among the general subject areas of courses taught by North-American systematic theologians; "Biblical Studies" (code level 4000) rank seventh. In our survey of dissertation topics (cf. Table 24, page 68a), the sciences of religion were found to rank fourth and biblical studies sixth; and in the study of graduate school areas of concentration, we found the sciences of religion ranking third and biblical studies again sixth. We said earlier that the relative high priority given to the sciences of religion during the formative stages in the educational process of systematic theologians was a sign of a general acceptance of the modern or "broader" understanding of the discipline, and that the relative low priority given biblical studies signified some continuing difficulties among contemporary systematicians in regard to establishing a positive relationship to biblical scholarship and to the discipline of biblical theology. In the present context, and in the light of the ongoing teaching programs of systematic theologians, these comments still seem valid. But several additional factors are involved, namely those that we have referred to in our analysis of the "range" of teaching (above, pp. 80 f.), "levels of teaching (above, pp. 83 f.), and "areas" of teaching (above, pp. 85 f.).

We found in these earlier contexts that considerable numbers of systematic theologians now teach in undergraduate institutions; that their teaching responsibilities include significant involvements in introductory-level courses; and that their areas of teaching generally span the spectrum from the principles of theology (methodology), through history of doctrine (dogmatics) and systematic (constructive) theology, to "other" subject areas. Obviously, since systematic theologians have had their teaching responsibilities broadened in these several ways, we can expect that there will be a similar broadening taking place in regard to subjects of courses, and especially that the sciences of religion (code level 3000) will tend to become more prominent in their course offerings.

This seems to represent an adequate explanation for the relative prominence of the sciences in the teaching of systematic theologians in North America. But it does not explain why biblical studies do not receive any similar degree of attention among the subjects they teach. Why is there not a single subject category from the 4000 level among the top 20 subject areas being taught by North-American systematic theologians? Can it be that biblical studies have now come to be considered so much a specialty, or that biblical theology has come to be so closely integrated with historical-critical biblical scholarship, that the teaching of biblical subjects is now generally considered the exclusive domain of the biblical scholars? Or has the systematic theologian for his part gone so far in attempting to relate his discipline to the secular sciences, the sciences of religion, or to historical studies, that he has lost consciousness of the primary root-age of systematic theology in biblical thought and is missing the aware-ness of his dependence on and interest in biblical studies?

We shall not attempt to answer these questions here; we will have occasion to return to them below, when we come to study the evaluative comments of systematic theologians themselves in regard to the current state of the discipline.

Sources of Teaching

The inquiry into the teaching programs of systematic theologians in North America would not be complete without some reference to the sources they use--the authors and works most often referred to as texts or required readings in the courses systematic theologians teach. In our questionnaire, we asked our respondents to list their major teaching texts or sources, and the vast majority did, providing us a very significant piece of information. In the DIRECTORY, the full bibliography thus pro-duced is included. It encompasses altogether 575 different authors and close to 1,000 different titles. Obviously, systematic theologians not only teach over a very wide spectrum of subjects; they also utilize a very wide spectrum of sources.

If one analyzes the bibliography of sources a little more closely, several interesting facts become evident; it is possible, for example, to undertake a quantitative ranking of authors as well as individual texts. Tables 30 and 31 (pages 93a and 93b) show the rankings, including the number of references obtained by each of the top 30 or so authors and each of the top 30 or so titles.

As Table 30 shows, topping the list of authors are the two major giants in 20th century systematic theology, Paul Tillich and Karl Barth--the references to Tillich outranking Barth's by a margin of 4 to 3. Next after the two giants comes a group of four contemporary writers--two Ro-man Catholics, namely, Karl Rahner and Bernard Lonergan, and two Protestants, namely, John Macquarrie and Wolfhart Pannenberg. Then, in 7th place comes the first of the old masters, Thomas Aquinas; others follow further down the list--Calvin in 9th place, Augustine in 19th (tied with Aulén and Schleiermacher), and Luther in 23rd place. But outrank-ing most of them are such 20th century authors as Gilkey, the Niebuhrs,

Table 30

Teaching Sources, Authors
(Number of syst. theols. referring to each)

Ranking		No. of References
1.	Tillich, SYSTEMATIC THEOLOGY, VOLS. I-III	36
2.	Macquarrie, PRINCIPLES OF CHRISTIAN THEOLOGY	25
3.	Gilkey, NAMING THE WHIRLWIND	18
4.	Lonergan, METHOD IN THEOLOGY	14
5.	Calvin, INSTITUTES, VOL. I-II	13
	Pannenberg, JESUS, GOD AND MAN	13
	Rahner, THEOLOGICAL INVESTIGATION, VOLS. 1-10	13
	Aquinas, SUMMA	13
10.	Kaufman, SYSTEMATIC THEOLOGY	11
11.	Latourelle, THEOLOGY OF REVELATION	10
12.	Aulén, THE FAITH OF THE CHRISTIAN CHURCH	9
	Cobb, LIVING OPTIONS IN PROTESTANT THEOLOGY	9
	Küng, THE CHURCH	9
	Tillich, DYNAMICS OF FAITH	9
16.	Moltmann, THEOLOGY OF HOPE	8
	Nichols, PELICAN GUIDE TO MODERN THEOLOGY, VOL. I	8
	R. Niebuhr, NATURE AND DESTINY OF MAN, VOL. I-II	8
19.	Hick, READINGS IN PHILOSOPHY OF RELIGION	7
	Hordern, LAYMAN'S GUIDE TO PROTESTANT THEOLOGY	7
	H.R. Niebuhr, CHRIST AND CULTURE	7
22.	Cobb, GOD AND THE WORLD	6
	Cone, BLACK THEOLOGY OF LIBERATION	6
	Cox, SECULAR CITY	6
	Gonzalez, HISTORY OF CHRISTIAN THOUGHT, VOLS. I-II	6
	Tillich, COURAGE TO BE	6
27.	Anderson, UNDERSTANDING THE OLD TESTAMENT	5
	Barth, EVANGELICAL THEOLOGY	5
	Brunner, DOGMATICS, VOL. I-III	5
	Bultmann, JESUS CHRIST AND MYTHOLOGY	5
	Fuller, FOUNDATIONS OF NEW TESTAMENT CHRISTOLOGY	5
	Long, SURVEY OF CHRISTIAN ETHICS	5
	Noss, MAN'S RELIGIONS	5
	Ogden, THE REALITY OF GOD	5

TABLE 31

Teaching Sources, Titles
(Number of systematic theologians referring to each)

Ranking		No. of References
1.	Paul Tillich	77
2.	Karl Barth	55
3.	Karl Rahner	46
4.	John Macquire	38
5.	Bernard Lonergan	34
6.	Wolfhart Pannenberg	33
7.	Thomas Aquinas	29
8.	Langdon Gilkey	23
9.	John Calvin	22
10.	H.R. Niebuhr	21
11.	Hans Küng	20
	Reinhold Niebuhr	20
13.	Rudolf Bultmann	19
14.	Emil Brunner	18
	Jürgen Moltmann	18
16.	John Cobb	17
17.	Gordon Kaufmann	16
	H. Schillebeeckx	16
19.	Augustine	14
	Gustaf Aulén	14
	Rene Latourelle	14
	Fr. Schleiermacher	14
23.	Avery Dulles	13
	Mircia Eliade	13
	Martin Luther	13
26.	Dietrich Bonhoeffer	11
27.	James Cone	10
	Yves Congar	10
	Gustavo Gutierrez	10
	Paul Ricoeur	10
	Piet Schonenberg	10
	Alfred North Whitehead	10

Küng, Bultmann, Brunner, Moltmann, Cobb, Kaufmann and Schille-
beeckx. The entire list forms a representative mixture of old and new,
Protestant and Catholic, European and American writers of theology.
It bears to be studied.

Interesting also is the listing in Table 31 of the single titles most
often referred to as sources for teaching, here ranked according to the
number of references obtained by each. Topping the list, again, is
Paul Tillich; the particular work most widely used as a textbook among
North-American systematic theologians in the 20th century is Tillich's
three-volume SYSTEMATIC THEOLOGY. Tillich is also represented by
two other works on this list, namely, DYNAMICS OF FAITH (ranked in
12th place) and COURAGE TO BE (in 22nd place). Next after Tillich's
major work come three works by contemporary authors that have a common
subject area, namely, theological method: Maquarrie's PRINCIPLES OF
CHRISTIAN THEOLOGY, Gilkey's NAMING THE WHIRLWIND, and
Lonergan's METHOD IN THEOLOGY. Tied for 5th place with works by
Rahner and Pannenberg are the only two classical systems of Christian
theology ranked on this list, Calvin's INSTITUTES and Aquinas' SUMMA.
The rest of the list is made up of systematic theologies such as Kaufmann's
(in 10th place), Aulén's (in 12th place), and Brunner's (in 27th place);
monographs on single doctrines such as Latourelle's THEOLOGY OF
REVELATION (in 11th place), Küng's THE CHURCH (in 12th place),
Niebuhr's NATURE AND DESTINY OF MAN (in 16th place), and Cobb's
GOD AND THE WORLD (in 22nd place); and general introductions to
theology such as Cobb's LIVING OPTIONS IN PROTESTANT THEOLOGY
(in 19th place), and Gonzales' HISTORY OF CHRISTIAN THOUGHT (in
22nd place). Again, the list bears close study.

Membership in Professional Societies

As a final detail in our picture of "the daily tasks" of systematic
theologians we shall look at the information we have received concerning
memberships in professional societies. Our interest here is primarily to inquire about the number of such memberships per systematic theologian and
to get an opinion as to which professional societies seem to be the most
common ones for the active professionals in this discipline to be members
of. Of the 560 persons included in the DIRECTORY 45 did not indicate
any active involvement in such professional associations at all. The rest
noted from 1 to 15 memberships, and altogether 235 different professional
societies were referred to. Tables 33 and 34 contain two different overviews of this material.

Table 33 (page 95a) is a graphic overview of the number of memberships in professional societies held by individual systematic theologians. As is evident from this graph, by far the greatest number of systematic theologians divide their loyalties between several different professional societies; the largest groups are clearly those who have memberships in 2 or 3 such societies, but significant numbers are members of 4 or 5 of them. The average for each person has been calculated at 2.79 professional society memberships.

Table 34 (page 95b) is a listing of the top 20 professional societies, ranked according to the number of systematic theologians who hold membership in each. Topping the list by a significant margin is the American Academy of Religion, with some 304 systematic theologians or 59.03% of the active professionals in the discipline in North America as members. No other single society comes close to the AAR in its role as a haven for scholarly interchange and professional dialogue in this discipline as in so many other fields. However, the rest of the list is also important, since, as we have seen, systematic theologians average some 2.79 professional society memberships. The variety is great, from denominationally oriented societies like the Catholic Theological Society of America, with 26.21% of all North-American Systematic Theologians as members, to special subject-oriented societies like the North-American Patristics Society, which has 1.55% of the systematic theologians in its membership. Particularly interesting is the fact that the list includes the American Philosophical Association, Society for the Scientific Study of Religion, American Society for Church History, and Society for Biblical Literature. When it comes to professional societies, obviously, North-American systematic theologians get around. Nevertheless, nowhere else do they seem to have found a meeting place and a forum as they have in the American Academy of Religion.

Table 33

Membership in Professional Societies, Systematic Theologians

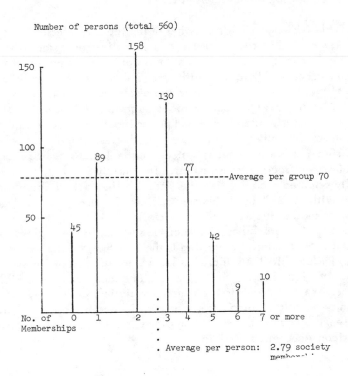

Number of persons (total 560)

158

150

130

100

89

77 ----------Average per group 70

50

45

42

10

9

No. of   0   1   2   .3   4   5   6   7 or more
Memberships

. Average per person: 2.79 society
membership

Table 34

Professional Societies, Number of Members
Among Systematic Theologians

Ranking	No. of Syst. Theols.as members	% of group*
1. American Academy of Religion	304	59.03
2. Catholic Theological Society of America	135	26.21
3. American Association of University Professors	75	14.56
4. College Theological Society	65	12.63
5. American Theological Society	57	11.07
6. American Philosophical Association	52	10.10
7. American Society of Christian Ethics	42	8.16
8. Society for Religion in Higher Ed.	41	7.96
Society for the Scientific Study of Religion	41	7.96
10. Canadian Theological Society	34	6.60
11. American Society for Church History	33	6.41
12. Society for Biblical Literature	28	5.44
13. American Catholic Philosophical Assoc.	20	3.88
14. Evangelical Theological Society	16	3.11
15. Catholic Biblical Association	13	2.52
Metaphysical Society of America	13	2.52
Religious Education Association	13	2.52
18. North American Academy of Ecumenists	11	2.14
19. Catholic Theology Society	10	1.94
20. American Society for Reformation Research	8	1.55
North American Patristics Society	8	1.55

*Total included: 515

Chapter 4

Systematic Theologians:
Research Interests and Publication Projects

We come now to that part of our inquiry which has to do with the growing edge of the discipline of systematic theology--the work that systematic theologians do to extend the body of knowledge in their discipline and lay the groundwork for future advances in their field--their research and publication projects. Our interest at this point focuses on three specific items in the biographies of systematic theologians contained in our DIRECTORY: the listing of their most recent publications; the information on the subjects and subject areas which fall within their general research interests; and the descriptions of the particular research and publication projects they are actively pursuing at the present.

In a sense, the material brought together in this chapter is that aspect of our study which comes closest to defining what is the lasting legacy of the present generation of systematic theologians in North America; it gives also the best indication to this point of what we can expect the orientation and sphere of interest of North-American systematic theologians to be in the forseeable future. Further details concerning this latter point are contained in SYSTEMATIC THEOLOGY TODAY, Part II.

Speaking of research and publications as the "growing edge of the discipline" puts this facet of the professional activities of systematic theologians in the proper context. In recent years, much negative publicity has befallen the formula "publish or perish," within the scholarly community and beyond--and rightly so. A hard and fast application of this principle, without regard for the individuality of scholars and without considering the many other facets of academic life and professional creativity which are involved in a scholar's total profile, is probably unwise. But in regard to the discipline of systematic theology as a whole, the principle is clearly sound. Without research and publication, the discipline--as a discipline of knowledge--would surely atrophy and deteriorate. From this perspective one could say that unless the active professionals in systematic theology continue their theological inquiries and publish their results, the discipline will perish. Research projects and publications are signs of health; they are indications that the discipline is still alive, still growing--or at least changing. They signify that the scholars in the field still feel there is significant work to be done-- or at least that work is still significant.

Whether the discipline is really developing or whether the work that is done is truly significant, are questions we must hold back for the moment, until we have had the opportunity to look at the facts.

Before we do that, there is one point that should probably be mentioned, since it bears on the evaluation of the material which will be presented here. It has to do with the nature of theology as a discipline of knowledge. Theology, by definition, is an endeavor in thought that is related both to faith and reason (theos and logos, or logic). It is conditioned both by a "word" or "story" or "message" which is recognized as the basis of meaning and the norm of truth, but it is conditioned as well by the language and thoughtforms which are characteristic of the mindset and culture within which it is done. There is, then, in theology, both an element of stability and an element of impermanence; theology is related to a Word that is considered permanent and absolute, but it uses words to express itself that are quite relative and changing.

In the light of this dual orientation of theology it is clearly to be expected that theological disciplines constantly undergo change. In fact, each of the disciplines of theology can be seen to take shape and develop through history by way of the dynamic interaction of faith and reason, tradition and culture. At times these disciplines are challenged to relate themselves to new developments in culture, knowledge and thought, generally; at other times they are challenged to take more seriously the essential content and meaning of the faith. The work of theology is therefore a continuing process--the responsible theologian is always existing at the crossroads of relevance and revelation.

We shall want to keep this dual dynamics in mind as we proceed to analyze the past publications, research interests, and active publication projects of North-American systematic theologians. Of particular interest here will be the impression this material conveys as to where in the dynamic cycle the systematicians in North America now seem to be--whether in the "outward" turn toward contemporary reason and culture or in the "inward" turn toward the content and meaning of the faith.

Past Publications

Our study has placed into focus the number and types of publications as well as the subject areas involved in this facet of the systematic theologians' work. We shall analyze these in turn.

As indicated in the introductory chapter of the DIRECTORY, it was necessary during the editing of that work to limit the number of publications which were to be listed. The limit was set at five, with the additional stipulation that the following order or priorities would be followed: first, books authored, starting with the most recent; second, books co-authored or edited, again starting with the most recent; third, chapters in books; and fourth, articles in journals, once more starting with the most recent. The edited material contained in the DIRECTORY is the basis for our analysis here; however, both because of the five item limitation and because in our present context we have not made an attempt to distinguish books authored, co-authored or edited, or to separate chapters in books and articles in journals, the following material is neither absolutely representative in numbers nor completely correct in regard to details.

Table 35 (pp. 99a and b) gives a series of summaries of the number and types of publications produced by systematic theologians in North America. Table 35A summarizes the number of items; 35B the types and distribution of items; 35C the total number of books; and 35D the total number of articles. The tables provide a wealth of information and will bear close scrutiny. We shall highlight only a few of the more interesting items here.

In Table 35A one notices that one fourth (25.36%) of all the systematic theologians in North America have not published any items that qualify for listing as professional contributions to their discipline. This is a surprisingly high percentage, especially in view of the fact that on the average these theologians have been active in the discipline some 13.51 years (cf. above, p.36a, Table 6) and are of an average age of 43.56 years (cf. above, p.31a, Table 1).

We notice on the other hand that a considerable number, namely 28.93%, have 5 or more published items to their credit. However, by far the largest number, 45.71%, are only now building their bibliographies, having from 1 to 4 items listed. Moreover, when the total number of items published by the entire group of systematic theologians in North America is calculated, it comes to only 1,411, which averages out to some 2.52 items per person--still a relatively low number for a professional group that has an average of 13.51 years of service and for whom publications are an important indication of professional accomplishment and academic maturity.

In Table 35B it is interesting to observe how the items are distributed--how many theologians are listed with books only, how many have articles only, and how many are listed with books and articles, and in what

Table 35

Number and Types of Publications, Systematic Theologians *

Table A – No. of Items:	No. of syst. theol.	% of total	Total of items
0 items	142	25.36%	
1 item	78	13.93%	78
2 items	65	11.61%	130
3 items	59	10.53%	177
4 items	54	9.64%	216
5 items or more	162	28.93%	810+
			1,411+

(average 2.52 per syst. theol.)

Table B - Types of Items:

I - Books only:	134	23.93%	
1 book	32	5.71%	32
2 books	23	4.11%	46
3 books	22	3.93%	66
4 books	11	1.96%	44
5 books or more	46	8.21%	230+
			418+
II - Combinations:	151	26.96%	
1 book, 1 article	18	3.21%	36
1 book, 2 articles	11	1.96%	33
1 book, 3 articles	12	2.14%	48
1 book, 4 articles (or more)	25	4.46%	125+
2 books, 1 article	8	1.43%	24
2 books, 2 articles	7	1.25%	28
2 books, 3 articles (or more)	29	5.18%	145+
3 books, 1 article	8	1.43%	32
3 books, 2 articles	20	3.57%	100+
4 books, 1 article	13	2.32%	65+
			636+

(cont.)

*Total number included: 560
+Calculated at the maximum of 5; not adjusted for "or more."

Table 35 (continued)

Table B - Types of Items (continued):

III -ᐧ<u>Articles only:</u>   133   <u>23.75%</u>

1 article	46	8.21%	46
2 articles	24	4.29%	48
3 articles	18	3.21%	54
4 articles	16	2.86%	64
5 articles or more	29	5.18%	<u>145</u>+
			357+

<u>Table C - Total Books:</u>   285   50.89%

0 books	275	49.11%	
1 book	98	17.50%	98
2 books	67	11.96%	134
3 books	50	8.93%	150
4 books	24	4.29%	96
5 books or more	46	8.21%	<u>230</u>+
			708+

(average 1.26 per syst. theol.)

<u>Table D - Total Articles</u>:   284   50.71%

0 articles	276	49.29%	
1 article	83	14.82%	83
2 articles	62	11.07%	124
3 articles	69	12.32%	207
4 articles	41	7.32%	164
5 articles or more	29	5.18%	<u>145</u>+
			723+

(average 1.29 per syst. theol.)

+Calculated at the maximum of 5; not adjusted for "or more."

99b

combination. The numbers are, in fact, roughly even: 23.93% are listed with books only; 26.96% have produced a combination of books and articles; and 23.75% have published articles only. Among those who are listed with books only (Table BI), the largest number (8.21%) have published 5 or more books; the rest shows a declining curve from the 5.70% who have published one book to the 1.96% who have published 4--an indication that book publishing is an increasingly tight game but that once a writer has broken through, he is likely to produce a goodly number of books (though our material does not allow us to study exactly how many, or to determine the full nature of the bibliography of people who have published 5 or more items). In the overview of those who have published a combination of books and articles (Table BII), we note that 11.77% are listed with one book in combination with varying numbers of articles; 7.18% have two books, plus one or two articles; and 2.32% are listed with four books and one article. Consistently, the greater numbers appear in the columns showing the total number of publications to be 5 or more--once again indicating that the publication business is rather selective but that those who succeed are likely to have repeated success. In the overview of those who have published articles only (Table BIII), the same observation is sustained, although here the largest number (8.21%) appears in the column showing those listed with a single article. Over the rest of the spectrum the pattern observed above is repeated--5.18% of systematic theologians being listed with 5 or more articles to their credit.

When we look more closely at the summary tables, Table 35C and D--C showing an overview of the total number of books listed, D analyzing the total number of articles listed--we are of course aware that the arbitrary 5-item limitation imposed on the listing in the DIRECTORY plays havoc with the numbers. This is particularly the case with Table D. Since articles were put in a second order of priority in the original listing, Table C is clearly more exact. Here we find that roughly half of all systematic theologians in North America (49.11%) have not published any books. Of the 50.89% who have, by far the largest percentage (17.5%) have published only a single volume--in many cases, actually, the doctoral dissertation--with declining numbers listed with two or three or four books and only 8.21% of all systematic theologians in North America having produced 5 or more books. The total number of books credited to the entire group within our study comes to 708, or an average of 1.26 book per theologian--a particularly dissappointing figure which may reflect not only the level of scholarship and literary productivity of active participants in the discipline but also the relatively small investment publishers are willing to make in publications by systematic theologians.

A second interest in studying the listing of publications by systematic theologians in North America is to gain an overview of the subjects or subject areas which have concerned these people in their research and publication   activities in the past few years. Such an analysis allows us to study the content priorities of these theologians and to compare the subjects of their publications with the subject orientation of various other facets of their work.

Table 36 (page 101a and b) is a presentation of the results of this overview, Part I focusing on the eight general subject areas, ranking them according to the number of references obtained by each area, Part II listing the individual subjects or subject areas that rank highest as having gained most attention in these publications. Altogether 1,338 subject references are included in this material; of the 143 subject codes included in our list of subjects, exactly 100 have been referred to in this context.

Table 36, Part I, reveals several important points. For one thing, by far the highest percentage of subject references fall within "Historical Studies" (code level 6000). This is quite in line with the tendencies we observed in connection with the dissertation topics of systematic theologians (cf. above, Table 24, p. 68a), but it seems to represent something of a reversal of the trend toward greater involvement in "Systematic/Dogmatic Subjects" (code level 8000) which we saw emerging in the analysis of these theologians' teaching areas (above Table 28, p. 87a). In the present context, however, we observe that "Systematic/Dogmatic Subjects" comes in as a strong number two, far stronger than this area has proved to be in any other context outside of teaching. In addition, the third place is taken by "Theological Studies" (code level 5000), making the combination of code levels 5000 and 8000 a stronger emphasis in the publications of systematic theologians than the leading single code level, 6000. Obviously, North-American systematic theologians are reaching toward a better balance between the "historical" preoccupations that characterized their educational programs and the "systematic" concerns that are central to their professional responsibilities.

An interesting point relates to the relative importance of "Practical Studies" (code level 7000) in the context of North-American systematic theologians' publications. This subject area ranks fourth on the list, significantly ahead of "Prolegomena" (code level 1000) and "Sciences of Religion" (code level 3000), and decidedly more central to the systematic theologians at this point than in any other context we have considered. The significance of this fact ought not to be overlooked, though its meaning is not immediately apparent. The importance of this subject area in this particular context may simply mean that systematic theologians are

Table 36

Subjects of Publications,
Systematic Theologians*
(Number of references to various subject categories)

Ranking	Code levels	Total	% of all sub. ref.**
I. General Areas:			
1. Historical Studies	6000	430	32.14%
2. Systematic/Dogmatic Sub.	8000	283	21.15%
3. Theological Studies	5000	171	12.78%
4. Practical Studies	7000	165	12.33%
5. Prolegomena	1000	133	9.94%
6. Sciences of Religion	3000	80	5.98%
7. Biblical Studies	4000	49	3.66%
8. Sciences in General	2000	27	2.02%
II. Specific Subjects, Subject Areas or Disciplines:* **			
1. History of Doctrine: Studies of Ind. Theologians	6370	211	15.77%
2. History of Doctrine: Motif Studies	6320	143	10.69%
3. History of Doctrine: Tradition Studies	6350	62	4.63%
4. Theological Methodology: Approaches to Theology	1220	60	4.83%
5. History of Doctrine: Comparative Studies	6380	59	4.41%
6. History of Doctrine: School Studies	6360	47	3.51%
7. Worship	7200	38	2.84%
8. Theology and Culture	5800	36	2.69%

(cont.)

*Total number included: 418
**Total number of references: 1,338
***Total numbers of subject codes: 143   Total referred to in this context: 100

101a

Table 36 (continued)

9. Theological Ideology	1500	31	2.32%
10. Doctrine of Church:			
Membership & Ministry	8530	27	2.02%
11. Social Ethics	5620	26	1.94%
12. Doctrine of Man	8232	26	1.94%
13. Moral Theology	5600	23	1.72%
14. Systematic Theology:			
Introductory Studies	5410	22	1.64%
15. Pastoral Theology	7400	15	1.57%
16. Theological Metaphysics:			
Theistic Studies	3510	20	1.49%
17. Doctrine of Christ	8300	20	1.49%
18. History of Doctrine:			
Period Studies	6330	19	1.42%
Contemporary Period	6335	19	1.42%
Ecumenics	7500	19	1.42%
Doctrine of Church:			
Means of Grace	8520	19	1.42%
Doctrine of Christian Life	8600	19	1.42%

required by present publishing policies to do their theology in such a way as to relate to the practical concerns of the church--that, perhaps, is where the publishing market is best at the present. However, the reason for the theologians' turn toward the "practical" subject areas may well be more profound. It may signify a conscious move on the part of professional systematic theologians to relate their discipline more directly to the life and work of the Christian community. If this is so--and, as we shall see when we come to analyze the self-evaluation of the active professionals in the discipline, it is--we have here a signpost showing the way to a closer integration of systematic theology and practical ministry, a development which augurs well for the future both for theology and for the church itself.

One disappointing feature in the overview of the subject areas of the publications of systematic theologians is the low ranking of "Biblical Studies" (code level 4000). Next to last on the list, this subject area is involved in only 3.66% of the publications listed. Once more our results are consistent with the general trends observed earlier. The disintegration of systematic theology and biblical studies is apparently far advanced, and there are few signs as yet that the breach between the two disciplines is being addressed by systematic theologians. As we shall see, systematic theologians are aware of the problem--one of their goals for the future is precisely the reintegration of systematic theology and biblical scholarship. But so far the r a p p r o c h e m e n t of the two fields of scholarship is still only a d e s i d e r a t u m on the agenda of systematic theologians; biblical scholars, with their new-found interest in biblical theology and "redaction criticism," seem to be well ahead of the systematicians in regard to bridging the gap between biblical scholarship and systematic theology.

We shall not make extensive analyses at this point of the rankings in Table 36 II of the individual subject categories which obtained the highest number of references in the publications of systematic theologians. There are few surprises in this list. Top honors, expectedly, go to "History of Doctrine: Studies of Individual Theologians" (subject code 6370). Other sub-categories of "History of Doctrine" follow in close order, although "Theological Methodology: Approaches to Theology" (subject code 1220) has broken into fourth place on the list and thus appears as the most important non-historical subject area in the publications of systematic theologians. In seventh place is "Worship" (subject code 7200), one of the sub-categories of "Practical Studies," ranked immediately ahead of "Theology and Culture" (subject code 5800). Other sub-categories of "Practical Studies" on the list are "Pastoral Theology" (subject code 7400), ranked 15th and "Ecumenics" (subject code 7500), tied for 18th place. Other sub-categories of "Theological Studies" on the list are 'Social Ethics" (subject code

5620), ranked 11th; "Moral Theology" (subject code 5600), in 13th place; and "Systematic Theology: Introductory Studies" (subject code 5410), ranked 14th. The top-ranking sub-categories of "Systematic/Dogmatic Subjects" is "Doctrine of Church: Membership and Ministry" (subject code 8530), ranked in 10th place on the list; "Doctrine of Man" (subject code 8232), tied for 11th; and "Doctrine of Christ" (subject code 8300), tied for 16th.

If we should ask, in the light of these inquiries, how systematic theologians now seem to be oriented, whether toward concerns for the content and meaning of the faith or toward concerns for contemporaneity and relevance, our material seems to give conflicting signals. The high ranking of "Historical Studies," "Systematic/Dogmatic Subjects" and "Theological Studies" indicate that systematic theologians now tend to give first priority to the content and meaning of the faith. But the strong emphasis which is given to "Practical Studies," "Prolegomena" (especially "Theological Methodology" and "Theological Ideology") as well as certain sub-categories of "Theological Studies" ("Theology and Culture," "Social Ethics" and "Moral Theology") seems to say that the concern for contemporaneity and relevance is also prevalent. Perhaps the conflicting signals are themselves indications that North-American systematic theologians are at the present experiencing the classical dynamics of theology: the tension between relevance and revelation, the interplay of LOGOS and logic. But that judgment must obviously be qualified by reference to the fact that "Biblical Studies" are still low on their list of priorities. All we can say in this context with regard to the general orientation of North-American systematic theology seems to be that a dynamic interplay is now going on between inquiries into theological traditions and attempts to come to terms with contemporary culture, church and society. Whether this process will result in theologies that are at one and the same time responsible conceptions of Christian essence and mature expressions of contemporary thought remains to be seen. It is clearly something we must leave to the next generation or two to judge.

Research Interests

In the questionnaire which was distributed to the professional systematic theologians in North America, and on which the biographical sketches in the DIRECTORY are based, respondents had opportunity to list the subjects or subject areas which fall within their general research interests at the present. Of the 560 systematic theologians listed in the

DIRECTORY, 511 provided the necessary information on this point, and they combined to make altogether 1,264 references to 115 of the 143 subject areas listed in our overview (pp. 15 ff., above). This gives an average of 2.29 subject references per person and an average of 8.84 references to each subject code on our list. Table 37 (p. 104a — b) is a summary of this material. Part I lists the general subject areas or groups of subjects ranked according to the number of references related to each code level; Part II lists the 20 or so top individual subjects or subject areas, ranked according to the number of references obtained by each subject code.

Table 37, Part I, shows several interesting things. The first is the fact that the general area of "Historical Studies" (code level 6000) is once more on top of the list. This confirms our observation in the previous section of a reversal of the tendency toward greater involvement in "Systematic/Dogmatic Subjects" (code level 8000) which we had found coming to the forefront in the analysis of subject areas of courses taught by systematic theologians. Although their teaching to a great extent related to the primary theological subject areas ("Systematic/Dogmatic Subjects" and "Theological Studies"), in regard to research interests they are once more engaged by the preoccupation with "Historical Studies" which characterized their dissertation research and dissertation topics during the final stage of graduate studies and which is evident in their past publications as well.

This impression is not altogether correct, however. Second and third on the list of research interests are the subject areas primarily related to theology--"Systematic/Dogmatic Subjects" (code level 8000) and "Theological Studies" (code level 5000)--and combined these two outrank "Historical Studies" by a little less than 7 percentage points. Also, we must observe that if the fourth and fifth-ranked subjects on the list are combined ("Sciences of Religion" and "Prolegomena"). these interests are generally on the level with "Systematic/Dogmatic Subjects," the second-ranked category. What we are seeing, in fact, is that the research interests of systematic theologians are on the whole better balanced in regard to the various major subject areas than any other facet of their activities which we have studied, including teaching. A closer comparison of Table 37 with Table 29 (p.88a) makes this more evident yet. While Table 29 shows the top four subject categories receiving 84.65% of all references in the context of teaching subjects, Table 32 shows the same four categories receiving 76.03% of all references in the context of research interests. The drop in references to "Systematic/Dogmatic Subjects" and "Theological Studies" is only 2.23%. The major part of the adjustment is therefore due to a significant increase in references to lower ranked general subject areas such as "Prolegomena," "Practical Studies," and "Sciences in General"--i.e., to the emergence of a better balance among all the major subject areas.

Table 37

Research Interests, Systematic Theologians
(Number of references to various subject categories)

Ranking	Codes	Total	% of all Sub. ref.
I. General Areas, Disciplines			
1. Historical Studies	6000	372	29.43%
2. Systematic/Dogmatic Sub.	8000	297	23.50%
3. Theological Studies	5000	161	12.74%
4. Sciences of Religion	3000	131	10.36%
5. Prolegomena	1000	125	9.89%
6. Practical Studies	7000	99	7.83%
7. Sciences in General	2000	40	3.16%
8. Biblical Studies	4000	39	3.09%
II. Specific Subjects, Subject Areas			
1. History of Doctrine: Studies of Ind. Theologians	6370	88	6.96%
2. History of Doctrine: School Studies	6360	58	4.59%
3. Doctrine of Christ	8300	51	4.03%
4. History of Doctrine: Motif Studies	6320	48	3.80%
5. Theological Methodology	1200	39	3.09%
6. Philosophy of Religion: Religious Language	3420	38	3.01%
7. Theology and Culture	5800	37	2.93%
8. Theological Methodology: Approaches to Theology	1220	35	2.77%
9. History of Doctrine: Tradition Studies	6350	34	2.69%
10. History of Doctrine: Area Studies	6340	33	2.61%

(cont.)

Table 37 (continued)

11.	Doctrine of Church	8500	31	2.45%
12.	Doctrine of Man	8232	29	2.29%
13.	Moral Theology	5600	25	1.98%
14.	Theology & Science, Technology	5700	24	1.90%
15.	History of Doctrine: Contemporary Period	6335	23	1.82%
16.	Theological "Ecology" (Context of Theology)	1400	22	1.74%
	Worship	7200	22	1.74%
18.	Social Ethics	5620	21	1.66%
	Means of Grace (Sacraments)	8520	21	1.66%
20.	Ecumenical Theology	7500	20	1.58%
	Interfaith Dialogue	7600	20	1.58%

A special feature which must be noted in Table 37, Part I, is that the general subject area "Sciences of Religion" (code level 3000) once more appears high in the rankings, namely in fourth place, and that "Sciences in General" (code level 2000) has here moved up a notch, ahead of "Biblical Studies." The broadening of the discipline of systematic theology which we observed in the context of graduate studies and teaching is thus apparently continuing. Systematic theologians in North America are clearly aware that their discipline cannot exist in isolation from the secular sciences or the scientific study of religion. In their research they not only involve themselves to a great degree in the natural sciences and in philosophical, literary, historical, psychological and sociological studies generally; they consider themselves to a great extent partners in all those disciplines which investigate the phenomena of religion in an empirical-historical manner. This could be good news and bad news for the discipline of systematic theology. On the one hand it seems to augur well for the integrative function of systematic theology—its ability to take into account the results of the different disciplines of study that have a bearing on the understanding and explication of faith; on the other hand it could signal a loss of vision on the part of systematicians—an abdication of their integrative role and a return to the rather more clearly delimited research projects that are characteristic of the "special" sciences. Both of these trends are in fact visible among North-American systematic theologians at the present, and which of them will prove to be the stronger is difficult if not impossible at this point to predict.

A third point which should be noted in reference to Table 37, Part I, is that "Prolegomena" (code level 1000), the general subject area that has to do with theological methodology, plays a much greater role in the research programs of systematic theologians than it has in any other facet of their work or their background to this point. This subject area ranks fifth in the listing of research interests and received 9.89% of all subject references—only a little less than the "Sciences of Religion" received. Systematic theologians are thus once more seen to be raising the fundamental questions as to the nature of theology, the relationship of theological disciplines, presuppositions for and approaches to theology, criteria for theology, theological authority, as well as questions having to do with the cultural context of theology, the point of view of theology, and the classification of theologies. This is undoubtedly important for the future of the discipline; it represents the kind of basic groundwork which has traditionally preceeded periods of gread advances for the discipline.

Important also is a fourth point that comes clear from the ranking of the research interests of systematic theologians, as it did in the previous analysis of their publications, namely, the relatively high level of interest in "Practical Studies" (code level 7000). This subject area ranks sixth among the research interests of systematic theologians, receiving 7.83% of all references listed. Though somewhat lower than the ranking this subject obtained in the previous section, the numbers still represent a significant increase compared with what we found in the analyses of teaching subjects and subject areas related to the systematicians' training or background, earlier. Apparently, systematic theologians are becoming more aware than they used to be of the relationship between their discipline and the practical aspects of church life and ministry, ecumenics and inter-faith dialogue. Significant numbers of systematic theologians now involve themselves in research programs designed to assist the church in developing a ministry, internally and externally, which is both theologically sophisticated and professionally competent, related in practice to the contemporary cultural, institutional, and human context of the church. All of which bears promise for the future both as far as the "practical" disciplines are concerned and as far as the relationship of theology and ministry is concerned.

One final point--a negative one--must be raised in connection with Table 37, Part I, namely, the fact that "Biblical Studies" (code level 4000) has dropped to last place in the ranking of general subject areas, garnering only 3.09% of the subject references in the context of the research interests of systematic theologians. This represents a further weakening of the relationship between systematic theology and biblical studies--already very tenuous, as we have seen--and it points to an almost complete bifurcation between biblical theology and systematic theology--a situation that is found to have very serious consequences for the discipline as a whole. We shall not speculate about the reasons behind these developments--we can do no better than raising the same questions which we stated in connection with the analysis of teaching subjects, above (p. 88a). This situation must, however, be of great concern to those who are aware of the foundational role of biblical studies, especially biblical theology, in systematic theology. If it is indeed a fact that biblical theology has become so closely integrated with historical-critical biblical scholarship as virtually to be considered a specialty uniquely reserved for biblical scholars, systematic theologians must seek to build a bridge to this sister discipline, if not by crossing over and involving themselves in biblical studies, then surely by establishing an open relationship with colleagues in biblical studies and inviting them to cross over and involve themselves in systematic theology.

When we come next to consider Part II of Table 37--the summary of the top 20 or so specific subjects and subject areas referred to in the listing of the research interests of North-American systematic theologians-- several important details are added to the picture. Not unexpected is the fact that the two specific subject areas receiving the greatest attention in

the research programs of systematic theologians are two sub-categories related to "History of Doctrine," namely "Studies of Individual Theologians"
(subject code 6370) and "School Studies" (subject code 6360). In fourth
place stands another such sub-category under "History of Doctrine," namely
"Motif Studies" (subject code 6320); in 9th and 10th places we find two
more, namely "Tradition Studies" (subject code 6350) and "Area Studies"
(6340); and in 15th place another, namely "Period Studies: Contemporary
Period" (subject code 6335). No other single subject category comes anywhere near the level of interest that "History of Doctrine" (subject code
6300) receives.

However, in third place over-all on the list of specific subjects receiving attention in the research interests of systematic theologians is one
of the central "Systematic/Dogmatic Subjects," namely, "Doctrine of
Christ" (subject code 8300). Other sub-categories of the 8000 code level
also obtain a fair amount of interest, namely, in 11th place "Doctrine of
Church" (subject code 8500), in 12th place "Doctrine of Man" (subject code
8232), and in 18th place "Means of Grace (Sacraments)" (subject code
8520). Apparently when it comes to the content of the Christian faith, the
systematic theologians of the last quarter of the 20th century seem to be
concerned with the same subjects which have engaged our predecessors
earlier in this century, namely Christology, ecclesiology, anthropology,
and sacramental theology.

Obvious from Table 37, Part II, is thirdly that the methodological
concerns are strong among the research interests of North-American systematic theologians. Not only is "Theological Methodology" (subject code
1200) ranked in 5th place over-all; other correlative subjects or subject
codes are high on the list as well--in 8th place "Approaches to Theology"
(subject code 1220), in 16th place "Theological Ecology (Context of
Theology)" (subject code 1400), and in addition certain parallel subject
areas within philosophy of religion and theological studies such as
"Religious Language" (subject code 3420), in 6th place; "Theology and
Culture" (subject code 5800), in 7th place; and "Theology and Science
(or Technology)" (subject code 5700), in 14th place. The clarification of
the nature of theology and the theologian's task in the modern age is clearly
a subject of high priority among North-American systematic theologians at
the present.

Finally, it is interesting to note the particular sub-categories of
"Practical Studies" which come to the forefront in the research interests of
systematic theologians. In 16th place on the list comes "Worship, Liturgy,
Spiritual Theology" (subject code 7200), and tied for 20th place "Ecumenics"
(subject code 7500) and "Inter-Faith Dialogue" (subject code 7600). Of a

distinctly "practical" nature are also the two sub-categories of "Theological Studies" which are ranked relatively high among the research interests of systematic theologians, namely, in 13th place "Moral Theology: Theological Ethics" (subject code 5600), and in 18th place "Social Ethics" (subject code 5620). We can thus observe that the systematic theologians of today do involve themselves in research programs that are related to the internal life of the Christian community, to the relationship between different religious communities--Christian and non-Christian--and to the ethical consequences of faith, generally and with specific reference to the contemporary social context.

Current Research
and
Publication Projects

We come now to the last of the items to be included at this point, the analysis of the subjects and subject areas of the research and publication projects North-American systematic theologians are currently pursuing. The information summarized here should give us the most detailed and up-to-date impression we can obtain of the directions of the discipline at the present time.

Table 38 (pages 108a & b) is a summary overview of this information, arranged in Part I according to the general subject areas, ranked according to the number of references to each area in the titles or descriptions of the projects listed in the DIRECTORY, in Part II according to the specific subjects, subject areas or disciplines which individually obtained the highest number of references. Of the 560 persons listed in the DIRECTORY, 98 or 17.5% listed no active research or publication project; the 462 who indicated an involvement in such projects combined to make 886 subject references. Of the 143 subject codes included in our master list, 107 are referred to in the material analyzed here.

Table 38, Part I, reveals several minor shifts of emphasis when compared with our earlier overviews of subjects of publications (Table 36, p. 101a) and research interests (Table 37, p. 104a). For one thing, "Historical Studies" (code level 6000 is now more entrenched than ever on top of the list, receiving more than a third (37.25%) of all the subject references in this context--a higher percentage than in any other context outside of dissertation subjects. Apparently, the tending of systematic theologians toward the history of doctrine or historical theology is the most pronounced characteristic of the discipline at the present time.

Table 38

Current Research and Publication Projects, Systematic Theologians*
(Number of references to various subject categories)

Ranking	Code levels	Total	% of all Sub. ref.**
I. General Areas			
1. Historical Studies	6000	300	34.25%
2. Systematic/Dogmatic Sub.	8000	169	19.29%
3. Prolegomena	1000	114	13.01%
4. Theological Studies	5000	113	12.90%
5. Sciences of Religion	3000	67	7.65%
6. Practical Studies	7000	65	7.42%
7. Sciences in General	2000	25	2.85%
8. Biblical Studies	4000	23	2.63%
II. Specific Subjects, Subject Areas or Disciplines:***			
1. History of Doctrine: Studies of Ind. Theologies	6370	90	10.27%
2. History of Doctrine: Motif of Studies	6320	64	7.31%
3. History of Doctrine: School Studies	6300	32	3.65%
4. History of Doctrine: Comparative Studies	6380	30	3.42%
5. Theological Methodology: Approaches to Theology	1220	29	3.31%
Doctrine of Christ	8300	29	3.31%
7. Theological Ideology (Point of View)	1500	27	3.08%
8. Theological Methodology	1200	24	2.74%
9. History of Doctrine: Tradition Studies	6350	23	2.63%
10. Doctrine of Man	8232	20	2.28%
			(cont.)

* Total number included : 462 (no projects reported 98)
** Total number of references: 876
*** Total number of subject codes: 143
Total referred to in this context:107

Table 38 (continued)

11.	Worship, Liturgy, Spiritual Theology	7200	18	2.05%
12.	History of Doctrine: Contemporary Period	6335	17	1.94%
13.	Philosophy of Religion Religious Language	3420	16	1.83%
	Moral Theology: Social Ethics	5620	16	1.83%
	Theology and Culture	5800	16	1.83%
	Doctrine of Church	8500	16	1.83%
	Means of Grace (Sacraments)	8520	16	1.83%
18.	Systematic Theology: Introductory Studies	5410	15	1.71%
19.	Moral Theology: Theological Ethics	5600	13	1.48%
20.	Philosophical Theology: Theological Metaphysics	3510	12	1.37%
	History of Doctrine: Area Studies	6340	12	1.37%
	Interfaith Dialogue	7600	12	1.37%

Still, we observe that "Systematic/Dogmatic Subjects" (code level 8000), though it has lost some ground relative to the other general areas-- reduced from 21.15% in the context of past publications and 23.50% in research interest to 19.29% in current research and publication projects-- is still in second place. If this subject area were to be combined with "Theological Studies" (code level 5000), these two categories are almost in balance with "Historical Studies" in the subjects of publication projects now under way among systematic theologians.

"Theological Studies" (code level 5000) appears to have kept a fairly constant grip on the attention of systematic theologians in all three contexts; the percentages are almost the same in each of the three overviews. However, this subject area is now no longer the third ranking area on the list; due to a dramatic rise in the interest in "Prolegomena" (code level 1000), "Theological Studies" is now reduced to fourth place in the rankings.

The prominence of "Prolegomena" in the current research and pub-lication projects of systematic theologians seem quite remarkable. The subject area has gone from fifth place in the earlier contexts, with percent-ages around 9.9, to third place in the present context, receiving 13.01% of all the subject references involved. Systematic theologians are appar-ently continuing to move in the direction of basic methodological concerns. This impression must, however, be qualified by reference to a corresponding. decline in the references to a closely related subject category, namely "Sciences of Religion" (code level 3000). This subject area has gone from a percentage of 5.98 in the context of past publications, to 10.36 in the context of research interests, to 7.65 in the present context. If we com-bine the percentages of these two general subject areas, the figures are al-most identical in the last two contexts (roughly 20%), somewhat higher than the percentage obtained in the context of past publications (roughly 15%).

What we see, then, at this point, is a trend toward a better balance in the discipline of systematic theology between historical con-cerns, interest in the content areas, and scientific, philosophical and methodological matters. The only areas which now lag behind are "Practical Studies" (code level 7000) and "Biblical Studies" (code level 4000). "Practical Studies" has gone from fourth place in the context of past publications, and a percentage of 12.33, to sixth place in the con-text of general research interests, with 7.83%, to sixth place in the con-text of current projects, with a percentage of only 7.42. "Biblical Studies" makes an even weaker showing; it has gone from seventh place in past publications, with 3.66% of all subject references, to last place in the last two contexts, with percentages of only 3.09 and 2.63, respectively.

What we earlier thought to be a trend toward the reintegration of systematic theology with the practical concerns of church and ministry seems thus to have evaporated in the contexts of general research interests and current research and publication projects. And the vacuum we have observed in regard to the involvement of systematic theologians in "Biblical Studies" seems to intensify dramatically.

In reference to Table 38, Part II--the analysis of the specific subjects, subject areas or disciplines which obtained the highest number of references in the context of current research and publication projects-- we shall limit ourselves to the following observations : Several sub-categories of "History of Doctrine" (subject code 6300) still dominate the top rankings on the list; in fact, the first four spots are taken by "Studies of Individual Theologians, " "Motif Studies," "School Studies," and "Comparative Studies," in that order. The top sub-category of "Systematic/ Dogmatic Subjects," namely "Doctrine of Christ" (subject code 8300), which in the context of general research interests was in third place overall, is now in fifth place, tied with "Approaches to Theology" (subject code 1220), a sub-category of "Theological Methodology." Other sub-categories of "Systematic/Dogmatic Subjects" among the top twenty or so subject categories are, in 10th place "Doctrine of Man" (subject code 8232) tied for 13th place "Doctrine of Church" (subject code 8500), and in the same bracket "Means of Grace (Sacraments)" (subject code 8520). Additional sub-categories of "Prolegomena" on the list are "Theological Ideology (Points of View)" (subject code 1500), in seventh place, and "Theological Methodology" (subject code 1200), in eighth. The top-ranking sub-category of "Practical Studies" is "Worship, Liturgy, Spiritual Theology" (subject code 7200), in 11th place. Among the sub-categories of "Theological Studies, " only "Moral Theology: Social Ethics" (subject code 5620), "Theology and Culture" (subject code 5800), and "Syst.Theol.: Introductory Studies" (subject code 5410) are on the list, namely, tied for 13th and in 18th place, respectively. The top-ranking sub-category in "Sciences of Religion" is "Philosophy of Religion: Religious Language" (subject code 3420), tied for 13th place.

In their responses to our questionnaire, several systematic theologians indicated that they are engaged in research and writing of systematic theologies, either one-volume works or multi-volume sets. In the light of this information we can expect in the next few years to see published a number of new theological "systems," from a variety of perspectives. The scholars engaged in such projects are Gabriel Fackre, Professor of Theology at the Andover Newton Theological School; Frederich Herzog, Professor of Systematic Theology at the Duke University Divintiy School; Boyd Hunt, Chairman of the Theological Studies Division of the Southwestern Baptist

Theological Seminary; Dale Moody, Joseph Emerson Brown Professor of
Systematic Theology at Southern Baptist Theological Seminary; Schubert M.
Ogden, Professor of Theology at the Perkins School of Theology, Southern
Methodist University; Harold H. Oliver, Professor of Philosophical Theology
at the Boston University School of Theology; and Herbert Richardson,
Professor of Theology at St. Michael's College, University of Toronto.

Overview of Subject References

Throughout this study we have applied a perspective that would
allow the practitioners of the art to tell us what the art is all about. As we
have seen, from the very beginning we opted for a definition of systematic
theology broad enough to include those concerned with "principles of
theology" (presuppositional studies, methodology), "dogmatics" (history of
doctrine), "systematic theology" (constructive theology, philosophical theology), as well as "other" correlative disciples (such as biblical theology,
moral theology, practical theology). In developing our overview of subject
areas--the major subject categories as well as the list of specific subjects,
subject areas or disciplines within each--we decided to do nothing more
than organize the information we had received as to the fields of interest
in which systematic theologians are in fact involved.

We discovered early a number of equivocations in the way terms
such as "dogmatics," "systematic theology," "symbolics," "principles of
theology," "philosophical theology," and "fundamental theology" are
used, and we decided therefore to employ certain general, descriptive
terms for the major areas of concern that seemed to fall within the purview
of systematic theologians, namely, "theological methodology" (principles
of theology, prolegomena), "historical theology" (history of doctrine,
dogmatics), "constructive theology" (systematics, philosophical theology),
and "other" concerns (to be specified and listed separately). It was as a
result of these procedures that the view developed that systematic theology
as it is practised today encompasses an entire spectrum of subject areas
which includes "Prolegomena," "Sciences in General," "Sciences of Religion," "Biblical Studies," "Theological Studies," "Historical Studies,"
"Practical Studies," and "Systematic/Dogmatic Subjects."

In our analyses above we have been particularly interested in
gauging the orientation of the displine as far as can be done on the basis of
the subject references which active, professional systematic theologians
have made in various contexts. We have analyzed each of these contexts

separately, only in a few instances making comparisons between the various contexts and commenting on what appeared to be trends or tendencies developing in the community of scholars in this field. Especially important, throughout, has been the question whether those now active in the discipline have managed to make manifest a reasonable balance between the many different concerns that fall within the interest sphere or intellectual perimeters of the discipline, as presently understood.

Having completed these analyses, we are now in a position to draw this entire material together in a final overview of subject references and to trace the subject orientation of North-American systematic theologians from the start of their educational process to the present stage of their academic careers. We are also at the point where we are finally able to raise the question of balance in the light of our study of the discipline as a whole.

Table 39 (pages 112a through d) is a presentation of the overview of subject references. It contains two parts: Part I is a listing of all the eight contexts studied and shows the percentages of subject references obtained by each of the major subject categories or code levels within each context. This table also includes several columns that show over-all percentages, over-all ranking, percentages for graduate/professional level involvements only (undergraduate majors excluded), and rankings for this level involvement specifically. Part II provides a series of graphs, one for each major subject area, showing the relative levels of interest--based on the percentages of subject references--across the spectrum of contexts studied. These charts and graphs bear considerable interest; a close study will be rewarding to the reader.

It is not our purpose here to offer any final evaluation of the discipline; the material we have submitted speaks for itself. Only a few comments must be added in the manner of clarification.

The only new information contained in Table 39, Part I, is in the columns showing over-all percentages and rankings, and in the columns showing percentages and rankings for graduate and professional level involvements only. The latter gives the most reliable picture of the relative strength of the various major subject areas within the discipline as such. However, as an overview of the kinds of studies that have contributed to the make-up of the mindset of contemporary systematic theologians in North America, the former columns are significant.

Over all as well as on the graduate/professional levels only, "Historical Studies" (code level 6000) and "Theological Studies" (code

Table 39

I. Subject Areas and Contexts
(by % of references) :

Codes: Subject Areas   Contexts *

	1	2	3	4	5	6	7	8	% overall (1-8)	Ranking (1-8)	%Grad. & Professional (2-8)	Ranking Grad. & Prof. (2-8)
1000 Prolegomena		0.58	0.31	3.06	5.30	9.94	9.89	13.01	5.26	6	6.01	5
2000 Sciences in General	87.60	5.05	8.77	1.18	1.57	2.02	3.16	2.85	14.03	3	3.52	8
3000 Sciences of Religion	7.09	5.24	14.46	2.94	10.49	5.98	10.36	7.65	8.03	5	8.16	4
4000 Biblical Studies	2.74	9.71	3.38	1.88	3.83	3.66	3.09	2.63	3.87	8	4.03	7
5000 Theological Studies	1.45	64.08	50.46	2.12	18.02	12.78	12.74	12.90	21.82	2	24.73	2
6000 Historical Studies	0.97	11.46	16.31	82.45	27.20	32.14	29.43	34.25	29.28	1	33.32	1
7000 Practical Studies	0.16	2.91	2.92	1.65	4.65	12.33	7.83	7.42	4.98	7	5.67	6
8000 Systematic/Dogmatic Sub.		0.97	3.38	4.71	28.94	21.15	23.50	19.29	12.74	4	14.56	3

(cont.)

* Key to Contexts:

1. Undergraduate Majors (Table 18, p. 54a)
2. Areas of Concentration, Seminary (Table 20, p. 57a)
3. Areas of Concentration, Graduate Programs (Table 22, p. 62a)
4. Dissertation Topics (Table 24, p. 68a)
5. Subject Areas, Teaching (Table 29, p. 88a)
6. Subjects of Publications (Table 36, p. 101a)
7. Research Interests (Table 37, p. 104a)
8. Current Research and Publication Projects (Table 38, p. 108a)

Table 39 (continued)

II. Graphs of Trends
(by % of references) :

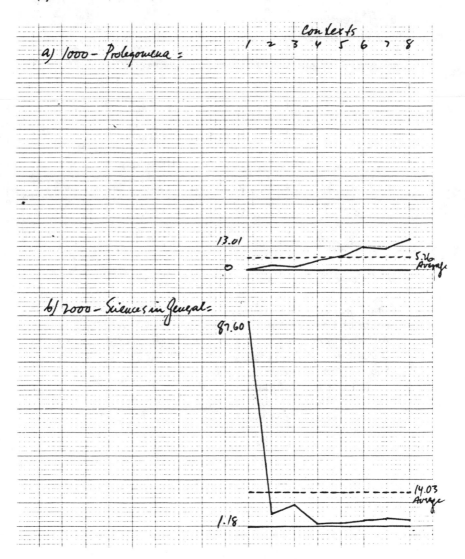

a) 1000 - Prolegomena :

Contexts
1 2 3 4 5 6 7 8

13.01

0   5.16
                                              Average

b) 2000 - Sciences in General :

87.60

                                              14.03
                                              Average

1.18

Table 39 (continued)

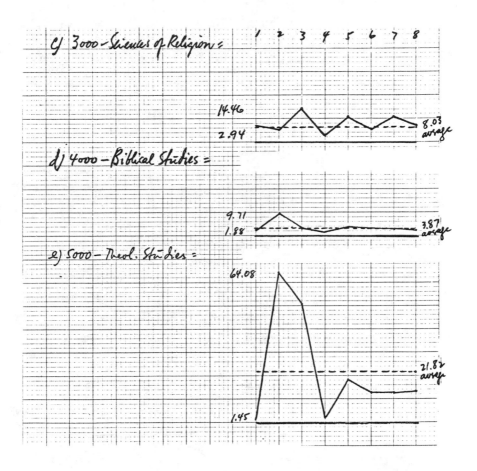

c) 3000 - Sciences of Religion =   1 2 3 4 5 6 7 8

14.46

2.94   8.03
                                           average

d) 4000 - Biblical Studies =

9.71
1.88   3.87
                                           average

e) 5000 - Theol. Studies =

64.08

                                           21.82
                                           average

1.45

Table 39 (continued)

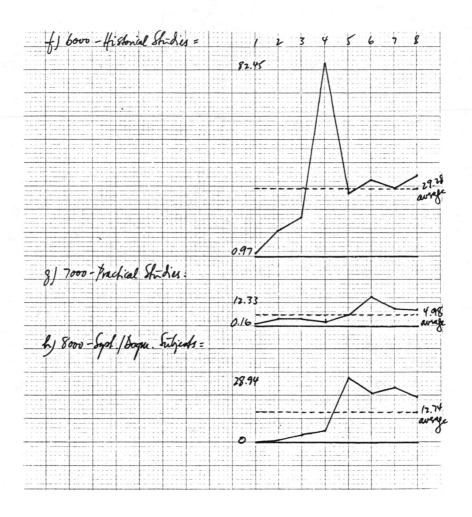

f) 6000 - Historical Studies =

g) 7000 - Practical Studies:

h) 8000 - Suppl./Bogus. Subjects =

level 5000) rank first and second, separated by some 7 to 9 percentage points. When undergraduate majors are taken into consideration, "Sciences in General" (code level 2000) comes in third; when this level of studies is excluded, this subject area falls into eighth place, and the rest of the subject areas move up a notch, with slightly higher percentages but keeping the same order. Over all, "Systematic/Dogmatic Subjects" (code level 8000) is fourth (for graduate/professional level involvements only, third); "Sciences of Religion" (code level 3000) fifth (fourth); "Prolegomena" (code level 1000) sixth (fifth); "Practical Studies" (code level 7000) seventh (sixth); and "Biblical Studies" (code level 4000) eighth (seventh). The percentages of subject references vary, in the over-all column from 29.28% for "Historical Studies" to 3.87% for "Biblical Studies", and in the graduate/professional column from 33.32% for "Historical Studies" to 3.52% for "Sciences in General."

Before raising the question of orientation and balance, a note in reference to the graphs in Table 39, Part II, is in order. These curves show how the eight major subject areas have fared, separately, over the spectrum of the systematic theologians' academic careers. Interesting in this context is the fact that only two subject categories show consistently rising curves, namely, "Prolegomena" and "Historical Studies." "Sciences in General" and "Biblical Studies," on the other hand, show downward trends and are very weak in comparison to other subject areas (except for the dominance of the former on the undergraduate level). Widely variant curves are exhibited by the subject areas of "Theological Studies" and "Systematic/Dogmatic Studies", though in the contexts that are related to the professional activities of systematic theologians the interest in these areas has clearly reached a level of constancy. The curve for the subject area of "Sciences of Religion" shows no tendencies to speak of, and "Practical Studies" shows no significant trend either.

In raising the question of balance, we do not of course expect that each of the eight major subject areas will be of equal importance to the discipline of systematic theology as a whole. Clearly, some of these areas are of primary or principal interest to systematic theologians, while others are of secondary or auxiliary importance. It is clear, moreover, that the eight general subject areas we operate with are not so defined as to be altogether comparable. Some of them can obviously stand on their own; others are more or less related, and some belong quite closely together. "Biblical Studies", "Historical Studies," and "Practical Studies" represent distinctly different facets of theology; "Theological Studies" and "Systematic/Dogmatic Subjects" are mutually interrelated. "Sciences of Religion" can easily stand as a separate category, but in our context it can also be related to "Prolegomena" and "Sciences in General." Other, more specific

113

correlations could be suggested, were we to consider the individual subject codes listed within each of the major subject areas in our overview.

If we can consider these kinds of correlations viable--if not inevitable--in this particular context, we discover that the discipline of systematic theology, as presently understood among North-American scholars in the field, encompasses five general spheres of interest:
- theological reflection
- historical investigations
- biblical studies
- practical/churchly concerns
- preparatory/methodological matters.

Two of these interest spheres would represent combinations of two or more general subject areas or code levels in our overview of subjects, namely, theological reflection (combining code levels 5000 and 8000) and preparatory/methodological matters (combining code levels 1000, 2000, and 3000). The rest correspond directly with a single code level or subject category in our overview.

If we proceed to calculate the sums of subject references related to each of these general spheres of interest, based on the percentages obtained from the next to the last column in Table 39, Part I (page 112a), the order of priorities and the relative strength of each interest sphere appears as follows:

1. theological reflection (code levels 5000, 8000)   39.29%
2. historical investigations (code level 6000)   33.32%
3. preparatory/methodological matters (code
   levels 1000, 2000, 3000)   17.69%
4. practical/churchly concerns (code level 7000)   5.67%
5. biblical studies (code level 4000)   4.03%

Clearly, the principal efforts of systematic theologians are focused on theological reflection and historical investigations of Christian thought. Relatively strong interests in pre-theological disciplines and methodological considerations undergird these efforts. As for practical concerns related to the life and ministry of the church and inquiries into the original sources of Christian faith and doctrine, systematic theologians apparently consider these more or less on the fringes of their discipline.

In sum, if the discipline of systematic theology is understood in the broadest sense as the study that brings into system all the considerations that have a bearing on the Christian understanding of things, it must be said that North-American systematic theologians are not yet at the point of fulfilling all their obligations.

This judgment gains further specificity when it is held against the background of the detailed analyses of the subject orientations of systematic theologians that we have undertaken in this volume. Our investigations have shown that the strongest single aspect of their work has to do with the historical study of Christian theologians and Christian thought. Constructive theology is being done, but only a relatively small portion of it focuses on the interpretation of central facets of Christian faith and doctrine, and very little aims toward a systemic, integrated explication of the faith. Considerable attention is being given to questions concerning the nature of theology, its relationship to culture, the sciences in general, and the sciences of religion, but its relationships to biblical studies and to the practical concerns of church life and ministry are not broadly considered or adequately explicated.

Clearly, the discipline of systematic theology has a considerable growing process to go through before it becomes in truth what it is in name.